AF817228

Treating Sexual Abuse and Trauma with Children, Adolescents, and Young Adults with Developmental Disabilities

TREATING SEXUAL ABUSE AND TRAUMA WITH CHILDREN, ADOLESCENTS, AND YOUNG ADULTS WITH DEVELOPMENTAL DISABILITIES

A Workbook for Clinicians

By

VANESSA HOUDEK, PSY.D.

and

JENNIFER GIBSON, PSY.D.

Advocate Health Care
Advocate Family Care Network
Childhood Trauma

CHARLES C THOMAS • PUBLISHER, LTD.
Springfield • Illinois • U.S.A.

Published and Distributed Throughout the World by

CHARLES C THOMAS • PUBLISHER, LTD.
2600 South First Street
Springfield, Illinois 62704

ISBN 978-0-398-09159-0 (paper)
ISBN 978-0-398-09160-6 (ebook)

With THOMAS BOOKS *careful attention is given to all details of manufacturing and design. It is the Publisher's desire to present books that are satisfactory as to their physical qualities and artistic possibilities and appropriate for their particular use.* THOMAS BOOKS *will be true to those laws of quality that assure a good name and good will.*

Printed in the United States of America
TO-C-1

Library of Congress Cataloging-in-Publication Data

Names: Houdek, Vanessa, author. | Gibson, Jennifer (Psychologist) author.
Title: Treating sexual abuse and trauma with children, adolescents, and young adults with developmental disabilities : a workbook for clinicians / by Vanessa Houdek, PSY.D. and Jennifer Gibson, PSY.D., Advocate Health Care, Advocate Family Care Network, Childhood Trauma Treatment Program.
Description: Springfield, Illinois : Charles C. Thomas . Publisher, LTD., 2017. | Includes bibliographical references and index.
Identifiers: LCCN 2016059547 (print) | LCCN 2017005274 (ebook) | ISBN 9780398091590 (paper) | ISBN 9780398091606 (ebook)
Subjects: LCSH: Sexual abuse victims--Rehabilitation. | Sexually abused children--Mental health. | Sexually abused teenagers--Mental health. |Adult child sexual abuse victims--Mental health. | Developmentally disabled. | Psychotherapy.
Classification: LCC RC560.S44 H68 2017 (print) | LCC RC560.S44 (ebook) | DDC 616.85/83690651--dc23
LC record available at https://lccn.loc.gov/2016059547

PREFACE

The Childhood Trauma Treatment Program (CTTP) has provided clinical services to child and adolescent survivors of sexual abuse and maltreatment since 1979 through Advocate Family Care Network (AFCN), a division of Advocate Health Care. Our mission is to assess and provide therapy and counseling for children, adolescents, and families that have experienced sexual abuse, maltreatment, psychological trauma, and sexual behavior problems, to teach clinicians to provide these services, and to prevent child sexual abuse through special workshops for adults. As a nonprofit agency treating trauma in the community for over 35 years, we became aware of a significant lack of knowledge, resources, and services for one of the most vulnerable populations: children, adolescents, and young adults with developmental disabilities who experienced sexual abuse.

CTTP provides three main functions in our community. First, we provide counseling and assessment services for children, adolescents, and families who experienced sexual abuse. Second, we provide training for adults in the community on ways to prevent and respond appropriately to child sexual abuse. Third, we train doctoral clinical psychology graduate students in the final year of their doctoral training in ways to assess and treat childhood trauma and abuse within a clinical setting to promote best practice skills in the field. While there are a number of prevention and intervention programs which exist to address sexual abuse in children, few to none address specialty considerations for people with developmental disabilities. As experienced providers in treating trauma and with the knowledge that individuals with developmental disabilities are at greater risk for experiencing sexual abuse but have limited treatment options, CTTP was compelled to create a user-friendly treatment manual for clinical professionals so that they may feel better equipped to treat children, adolescents, and young adults with developmental disabilities who experienced sexual abuse. Additionally, this clinical workbook provides information related to more general trauma treatment as well as prevention of sexual abuse in this vulnerable population. Currently, there are very limited trauma treatment resources for these individuals. We hope our efforts increase and enhance this extremely important and under-researched area and assist others as we continue our mission together to treat and prevent child sexual abuse in our communities.

INTRODUCTION

If you are reading this workbook, you are likely looking for guidance or finding a lack of knowledge, resources, and skills within the community to best approach sexual abuse and trauma treatment with children, adolescents, and young adults with developmental disabilities. Our ultimate goal with the creation of this workbook is to promote a standard in the field for clinicians to increase confidence, competence, and effectiveness in addressing child sexual abuse and trauma treatment with children, adolescents, and young adults with developmental disabilities. The treatment model presented in this workbook may be easily referred to as Trauma Treatment for Children, Adolescents, and Young Adults with Developmental Disabilities (TT-CAYDD).

We hope that this workbook is used as a guide for masters and doctoral-level clinicians who are either licensed or are in-training and under the supervision of a licensed mental health professional. The workbook is divided into two parts: the first part is focused on research and education regarding trauma treatment, developmental disabilities, and our module for treatment within this population while the second part of the workbook presents examples of interventions, worksheets, and therapeutic activities for use with clients. The second part is meant as a supplement to part one and is not an exhaustive list of interventions, worksheets, or therapeutic activities that can be utilized to achieve similar goals in treatment. This workbook can be used flexibly with clients as modules within the treatment can be utilized in varying orders or omitted as appropriate. For example, the module on sexual behavior problems will not apply to all children, adolescents, and young adults seeking trauma treatment. We do suggest that psychoeducation modules occur within the beginning of treatment, coping skills within the middle phase, and trauma narratives toward the end of treatment.

Throughout this manual we utilize the term "survivor" to denote any individual who experienced sexual abuse rather than the term "victim." Our hope is that individuals will feel empowered by this term; however, we acknowledge that surviving sexual abuse is not synonymous with healing from sexual abuse. Many individuals have engaged in long-term counseling services or other healing practices and have not only survived abuse but are now thriving. It is our hope that all survivors thrive.

We utilize the term "developmental disability" through this manual. A variety of disorders and conditions apply to this category. Disorders such as Cerebral Palsy, Down Syndrome, Autistic Spectrum Disorders, Attention Deficit/Hyperactivity Disorder (ADHD), Nonverbal Learning Disorder, and

Fetal Alcohol Syndrome or Effects are reviewed in this manual. Additionally motor, communication, sensory, and feeding problems are briefly discussed. It is important to note that developmental disorders each lie on a wide spectrum of functioning level and severity and by no means, are the disorders discussed in this manual representative of all developmental disabilities. This manual is not intended to provide detailed information on all developmental disabilities but rather provide a general overview of more common developmental disorders to increase understanding of assessment and treatment interventions discussed. It is intended for use with individuals with a moderate to high functioning level. Clinicians must consider the functioning and developmental level of each individual and the appropriateness of interventions.

CONTENTS

Page

Preface v

Introduction vii

Chapter

PART I: CLINICAL CHAPTERS FOR CLINICIANS

1. Sexual Abuse (SA) and Trauma 5
    - Defining Sexual Abuse 5
    - Prevalence of Sexual Abuse 6
    - Common Risk Factors 6
    - Pregnancy, Sexually Transmitted Infections (STI), and General Medical Concerns 7
    - General Psychological Distress 9
    - Depression and Suicidality 9
    - Substance Abuse 10
    - Anxiety and Posttraumatic Stress Disorder (PTSD) 10
    - Nonsuicidal Self-Injury (NSSI) 10
    - Disordered Eating. 11
    - Guilt and Shame 12
    - Academic and Vocational Problems 12
    - Behavioral Difficulties 12
    - Revictimization 13
    - Intimate Relationships 13
    - General Protective Factors 14

2. Brief Overview of Developmental Disabilities (DD) 15
Borderline Intellectual Functioning. 15
Down's Syndrome 16
Cerebral Palsy (CP) 16
Nonverbal Learning Disorder (NVLD) 16
Autism Spectrum Disorder 17
Attention Deficit/Hyperactivity Disorder (ADHD) 17
Fetal Alcohol Effects 17
Additional Considerations 18
3. Assessment and Treatment Guidelines For Children, Adolescents, and Young Adults With Developmental Disabilities Who Experienced Sexual Abuse 19
General Guidelines for Trauma-Informed Assessment with Children, Adolescents, and Young Adults with Developmental Disabilities 19
General Guidelines for Trauma-Informed Treatment with Children, Adolescents, and Young Adults with Developmental Disabilities 23
4. Trauma Treatment Models and Preparing for Trauma Treatment . . . 27
Trauma-Focused Cognitive-Behavioral Treatment (TF-CBT) 27
Integrative Treatment of Complex Trauma (ITCT) 28
Preparing for Trauma Treatment 29
5. Trauma Treatment with Children, Adolescents, and Young Adults with Developmental Disabilities- (TT-CAYDD) 31
Psychoeducation 31
Affect Regulation (Identification and Modulation) 32
Cognitive 32
Coping Skills 33
Self-Awareness and Mindfulness 34
Social Skills/Healthy Relationships. 34
Sexuality and Sexual Behavior Problems. 35
Sexual Behavior Problems 36
Sex Education/Body Awareness 36
Safety Skill Training. 37
Trauma Story 37

6. Caregivers 39
Define Caregiver Role: Advocate, Liaison, Collaborator 39
Self-Care 39
Participation in Treatment 40
The Role of Schools: Resources, Accommodations 40
Family Support 41
7. Adjunct Treatments and Services 43
Evaluation/Testing 43
Group Therapy 43
Psychiatric Services and Level of Care (LOC) 44
Occupational/Physical Therapy 44
Speech Therapy 45
School Counselors and Social Workers. 45
Medical 45
Animal-Assisted Therapy. 46
Therapeutic Massage/Yoga 46
Chapter 8. Prevention Strategies 48

PART II: THERAPEUTIC WORKSHEETS, ACTIVITIES AND INTERVENTIONS FOR TT-CAYDD

Introduction to Worksheets 53
Psychoeducation Worksheets 55
Affect Regulation (Identification and Modulation) Worksheets. 71
Cognitive Worksheets 81
Coping Skills Worksheets 99
Self-Awareness and Mindfulness (Worksheets) 105
Trauma Story (Worksheets) 111
Social Skills/Healthy Relationships (Worksheets). 121
Sexual Behavior Problems (Worksheets) 135
Sex Education /Body Awareness (Worksheets) 145
Safety Skills Training (Worksheets) 157

Appendix: Additional Resources 163
References 167
Index. 171

Treating Sexual Abuse and Trauma with Children, Adolescents, and Young Adults with Developmental Disabilities

Part I

CLINICAL CHAPTERS FOR CLINICIANS

Chapter 1

SEXUAL ABUSE (SA) AND TRAUMA

Sexual abuse can have devastating effects on an individual. Painful and challenging internalizing and externalizing behaviors can result from abusive experiences. Internalizing issues are defined as psychological problems that cannot be more easily seen by others such as depression, suicidality, anxiety disorders, posttraumatic stress disorder, guilt and shame. Externalizing behaviors are defined as behaviors that are more easily observed by others which include aggression, behavioral disorders, substance abuse or dependence, and sexual risk taking. Some consequences of sexual abuse can be defined as both internalizing and externalizing, such as eating disorders and nonsuicidal self-injury since the emotional distress is unseen to others yet the physical symptoms (e.g., low body weight, scarring) can be apparent. Relationships can suffer as survivors may struggle with trust, intimacy, and sexual relations. Additionally, survivors may suffer from negative health outcomes because of abuse, which can include chronic pain syndrome, fibromyalgia, and somatic complaints. These are only a few examples of how a person's physical health may deteriorate because of sexual abuse. Sexual abuse among people with developmental disabilities is not well-researched; however, the research that is available indicates that individuals within this population experience similar effects to children and adolescents within the general population. Clinicians must consider the individual's level of functioning to determine appropriateness of each intervention.

Defining Sexual Abuse

Defining what constitutes sexual abuse is not an easy task and there is continued debate among professionals. Individuals in a variety of fields, such as medical, psychology, anthropology, and sociology, have produced various definitions of abuse (Haugaard, 2000). One issue is the age-range the term "childhood" covers, which may include anyone under 18, 17, or 16 years old depending on the study and/or researcher (Haugaard, 2000). This age range may expand to older ages when working with individuals within the developmentally disabled population due to various impairments which may limit the ability for a young adult with a developmental disability to consent to sexual activity. The World Health Organization uses the term "sexual violence," which is defined as "any sexual act, attempt to obtain a sexual act, unwanted sexual comments or advances, or acts to traffic, otherwise directed, against a person's sexuality using coercion, by any person regardless of their relationship to the victim, in any setting, including but not limited to home and work" (World Health Organization. (WHO), 2002, p. 149). Although there is debate among the field in regards to what constitutes sexual abuse, understanding the prevalence, risk factors, consequences, and protective factors regarding sexual abuse is extremely important to help survivors heal and prevent future abuse.

Prevalence of Sexual Abuse

Since there is debate among what constitutes sexual abuse, rates of occurrence are likely lower than actual rates of abuse. In addition, many abuse cases go unreported due to the survivor feeling ashamed or fearful of telling, especially if the perpetrator is a family member or trusted adult. Individuals with developmental disabilities may struggle to communicate abusive experiences to trusted adults or authorities due to communication or cognitive difficulties. Research has shown that 1 in 10 children are sexually abused before 18-years-old (Townsend & Rheingold, 2013). The researcher Sobsey (1996) reported that individuals with disabilities are at a much greater risk, over four times as likely, to be victims of crime than individuals without disabilities. Sullivan and Knutson (1998) further found that children with communication disorders were more likely to be physically and sexually abused. Sexual abuse is unfortunately not a rare experience. Sexual violence occurs at high rates all over the world, including in the United States. With such high prevalence rates, understanding risk and protective factors as well as the consequences of abuse is paramount to helping abuse survivors heal and protecting potential abuse victims.

Common Risk Factors

There are a multitude of common risk factors for sexual abuse within the general population; however, children and adolescents with developmental disabilities are at increased risk for a variety of reasons (Ryan, 1994). According to the National Child Traumatic Stress Network (2004), the federal definition of a developmental disability is "a severe, chronic disability that is attributable to a mental or physical impairment or combination of both, occurs prior to 22 years of age, and results in functional impairments in a variety of activities." Examples of functional impairment domains include self-care, mobility, or communication. Research has estimated that individuals with disabilities are 2 to10 times more likely to be sexually abused than individuals in the general population (Westat Inc., 1993).

Unique risk factors for sexual abuse for individuals with developmental disabilities include the types and levels of functional impairment in the individual as well as exposure to varying levels of care by a variety of institutions. Sobsey and Doe (1991) reported that the risk of abuse increases by 78 percent for individuals with developmental disabilities due to exposure to institutions and service systems. Children and adolescents with developmental disabilities may be dependent on caregivers for basic needs and become more vulnerable to abuse and less likely to report abuse by a caregiver or adult he or she depends on for basic needs.

Children and adolescents with developmental disabilities are less likely to receive appropriate sexual education or information regarding healthy sexuality. This limited knowledge increases the general risk to this population, and if combined with cognitive or social skill impairments, increases the ability for perpetrators to normalize inappropriate sexual behaviors or confuse and manipulate these individuals. Thus, individuals with developmental disabilities are often targeted by perpetrators.

Due to these risk factors, legally prosecuting offenders can be difficult which further increases the general risk to this population. Offenders may feel as if they can "get away" with this crime due to the individual's level of functioning, communication issues, mobility issues, or a variety of other impairments.

The National Child Traumatic Stress Network (2004) reported that children and adolescents with developmental disabilities have limited protective factors, in comparison with the general population, to counteract the unique risk factors of this population. The consequences of sexual abuse may vary from person to person but it is important to note that the following topics may or may not apply to individuals within the developmentally disabled population as the vast majority of research is conducted with individuals without developmental disabilities.

Pregnancy, Sexually Transmitted Infections, and General Medical Concerns

Medical concerns, such as unwanted pregnancies and sexually transmitted infections are consequences associated with experiencing sexual assault or abuse. Unwanted pregnancies as the result of sexual assault occur in 5 percent of women; in the United States this equates to more than 32,000 pregnancies among survivors between 12-45 years old (WHO, 2002). Because they feel a lack of control, adolescent survivors of sexual abuse are more likely to participate in sexually risky behaviors (e.g., not using contraceptives) and become pregnant or contract a sexually transmitted infection (STI) or Human Immunodeficiency Virus (HIV: WHO, 2002). Survivors may feel a lack of control because they were unable to control the abuse they suffered. This may in turn lead to individuals acting out and putting themselves in other situations in which they have no control, such as not using protection and becoming pregnant or being infected with a STI.

Transmittal of an STI and/or HIV is a devastating consequence of sexual assault. STI and HIV transmittal occur more frequently during forced encounters than consenting sexual relationships because of the violence associated with assault; generally, there are multiple cuts that occur, which increases the risk of transmittal (WHO, 2002).

Increased risk of medical problems is also a consequence of sexual abuse. Sachs-Ericsson, Blazer, Plant, and Arnow (2005) conducted a study with over 5,000 participants to determine medical problems associated with sexual and physical abuse a year after the trauma. Independent of physical abuse and psychiatric disorders, survivors of childhood sexual abuse suffered from increased medical concerns, such as chronic pain, fatigue, autoimmune disorders, and sleep disorders. The combination of physical and sexual abuse did not result in a higher frequency of medical problems. This means that sexual abuse alone caused a significant amount of medical difficulties regardless of the presence of physical abuse. Sexual abuse can cause high instances of medical problems even after the abuse occurs. For example, a survivor may develop a chronic pain disorder months or even years after the abuse occurs. Unfortunately, many of the medical problems that develop continue into adulthood.

Unwanted pregnancies, STI or HIV infections, and medical conditions are all possible consequences of abuse. Along with specific medical consequences of abuse, such as a chronic pain disorder, abuse survivors may experience an overall decrease in their health leading to increase in general medical concerns. This may include enuresis and encopresis, especially in children. Enuresis and encopresis is when a child, adolescent, or young adult either involuntarily, or voluntarily, voids their bladder or has a bowel movement, following a period of time in which that individual had developmentally age-appropriate toileting skills. This can occur at night, such as bedwetting, as well as during the day.

General Psychological Distress

Many survivors of sexual abuse suffer from long-term psychological distress, which often can extend far into adulthood. Long-term psychological distress refers to extended periods of time the individual experiences a decrease in their overall mental health. Kallstrom-Fuqua, Weston, and Marshall (2004) studied a group of low-income women who were sexually abused as children or adolescents. Several factors were found to determine the level of distress experienced by survivors including the level of force, number of perpetrators, relationship to perpetrator, and age at first assault; however, the relationship between sexual abuse and psychological distress was mediated by feelings of powerlessness and stigmatization. This research suggests that when individuals are severely abused and feel powerless to stop the abuse as well as experience immense shame about the abuse, they are most likely to experience significant psychological distress. General psychological distress may lead to other mental health issues, such as depression.

Depression and Suicidality

Depression and suicidality are common consequences of experiencing sexual abuse. Suicidality refers to suicidal desires, thoughts, plans, or attempts. Kaplow and Widow (2007) found that maltreated youth, which included a category for sexual abuse, predicted later depression and anxiety symptoms in adulthood compared to a youth who did not suffer abuse. If the abuse occurred later in childhood (up to age 12) the individual was more likely to have behavioral issues as an adult (Kaplow & Widow, 2007). Abuse survivors had a higher chance of developing depression and anxiety as adults as contrasted with individuals who had not suffered abuse. Also, if abuse occurred during late childhood the survivor was more likely to have behavioral problems in adulthood, such as substance abuse.

Read, Agar, Barker-Collo, Davies, and Moskowitz (2001) studied the relationship between childhood sexual abuse and suicidality. Using case files of an outpatient population, results indicated that childhood sexual abuse was associated with previous psychiatric hospitalizations, younger ages of psychiatric hospitalization, and past and present suicidality. In fact, being a survivor of childhood sexual abuse was a better predictor for current suicidality than the presence of depression, meaning that childhood sexual abuse was more influential in later feelings or attempts of wanting to kill oneself than depression.

In sum, survivors of childhood sexual abuse are not only more likely to be depressed but also more likely to attempt suicide or have thoughts of suicide. They are also more likely to be hospitalized in a psychiatric facility due to depression or suicidality.

Substance Abuse

Substance abuse is a maladaptive coping strategy many survivors utilize to manage or attempt to forget sexual traumas. Substance abuse can include inappropriate use of alcohol, prescription medications, or over the counter medications as well as illegal use of drugs such as heroin or cocaine. Survivors of sexual abuse are at an increased risk of abusing substances or becoming addicted to alcohol or drugs. Spatz, Widom, Marmorstein, and Raskin (2006) studied over 800 survivors of abuse and found that survivors are 1.5 times more likely to abuse illegal drugs than individuals without a history of abuse and that this pattern of behavior extended into middle adulthood. As discussed earlier, substance abuse increases the risk an individual will experience a sexual assault, leading to a vicious cycle of survivors abusing alcohol or drugs to escape what happened to them and increased exposure to risky and dangerous situations which may increase the likelihood of future assaults.

Anxiety and Posttraumatic Stress Disorder (PTSD)

Anxiety is also apparent in sexual abuse survivors, specifically regarding posttraumatic stress disorder (PTSD). PTSD is defined by three core symptoms, including hyper-arousal (intensified awareness of one's external surroundings and internal cues, such as heart rate), avoidance (attempts to get away from anything that reminds the individual of the assault), and re-experiencing (feelings that the event is reoccurring, such as flashbacks) of the traumatic event. Children or adolescents can experience PTSD symptoms into adulthood. Rodriguez, Ryan, Vande Kemp, and Foy (1997) studied posttraumatic symptoms of survivors of childhood sexual and physical abuse. These researchers found that instances of PTSD increased when physical abuse was also present. Individuals who suffered sexual and physical abuse were at an increased risk of experiencing anxiety or PTSD. Survivors of sexual abuse were at an increased risk for developing anxiety problems or PTSD when compared to individuals who had not experienced abuse.

Nonsuicidal Self-Injury (NSSI)

Nonsuicidal self-injury (NSSI) refers to when an individual intentionally harms their body, such as cutting their arm with a razor, with the intent to feel pain but not as an attempt to commit suicide. To most people, the notion of someone who is not suicidal but harms oneself does not make sense. NSSI is a maladaptive coping strategy survivors may utilize to manage painful internal experiences. Traumas can cause an individual to become "emotionally numb" meaning that they have difficulty experiencing both positive and negative emotions. Feeling pain from NSSI allows the person to not only feel an emotion but reminds them that they are alive, whereas traumas can make a person feel empty and dead inside.

Weierich and Nock (2008) studied PTSD symptoms and NSSI in a group of childhood sexual abuse survivors. Results indicated a significant association between childhood sexual abuse, PTSD, and NSSI. Survivors of childhood abuse are likely to experience not only PTSD but also engage in NSSI. One possible reason for this relationship can be explained by the symptom of re-experiencing the trauma in PTSD. Often, survivors engage in NSSI to avoid or reduce tension resulting from the trauma, especially when they begin to have flashbacks of the trauma. The pain felt from NSSI allows the survivor to feel something different than how the trauma made them feel. Additionally, for survivors whose emotions have gone "numb" the pain reminds the survivor that they are alive and can feel something.

Disordered Eating

Disordered eating as well as eating disorders can be consequences of sexual abuse, which allows survivors to use food to control or escape their trauma. Disordered eating can be defined as unhealthy eating patterns or an unhealthy relationship with food. Eating disorders are generally defined by a set of symptoms related to food that create poor functioning in the individual. Hund and Espelage (2005) found that childhood abuse survivors were more likely to exhibit psychological distress and alexthymia (difficulty describing emotions), which increased rates of disordered eating. Thus, survivors have higher levels of general psychological distress and difficulty emotionally expressing themselves which can lead to unhealthy relationships with food. According to research, sexual abuse is a common risk factor for multiple eating disorders, such as anorexia nervosa, bulimia nervosa, and binge-eating disorder (Jacobi, Hayward, De Zwaan, Kraemer, & Agras, 2004). These disorders involve patterns of not eating, restricting calories excessively, an overconcern with weight and body image, vomiting meals, abusing laxatives, or other methods of purging calories from the body. In addition, the disorders may involve periods of overeating excessive amounts of food. It is likely that these attempts to regulate food intake are related to issues of control; for survivors, it may be that they begin to control food because they felt so out of control during the abuse and food is a factor in their life they can control.

Guilt and Shame

Many survivors of childhood or adolescent sexual abuse experience guilt and shame regarding the trauma. Often, survivors engage in self-blame, that is, feeling that they either caused the abuse or could have done something to stop the abuse but did not. Wyatt and Newcomb (1990) studied a sample of 111 survivors of sexual abuse to examine the relationship between sexual abuse and long-term negative consequences of abuse. Researchers found that if a survivor engaged in self-blame than they were more likely to experience negative consequences because of the abuse, such as interpersonal problems. Thus, when survivors feel responsible for either the abuse or not stopping the abuse they are more likely to experience the consequences of abuse such as depression and suicidality, substance abuse, anxiety and PTSD, general medical and psychological distress, NSSI, and disordered eating.

Academic and Vocational Problems

Academic problems arise for adolescent survivors of abuse. Examples of academic problems include poor grades and inconsistent attendance or truancy. Eckenrode, Laird, and Doris (1993) reviewed the school and social service records of over 400 abused or neglected adolescents. Abused or neglected adolescents were found to perform significantly below same-aged peers who had no history of abuse or neglect; specifically regarding standardized tests and grades. Survivors had lower grades and lower scores on standardized tests when compared to individuals who did not suffer sexual abuse. Additionally, abused or neglected adolescents were more likely to fail a grade in school. Abused adolescents were more likely to also exhibit behavioral problems in school when compared to neglected children. In sum, survivors are more likely to have poorer grades, fail a grade, and behaviorally act out in school.

Children and adolescents within the developmentally-disabled population generally receive special education services and accommodations within academic settings, so academic difficulties may be difficult to discern in this population. Additionally, older adolescents and young adults may be involved in vocational programs which may also be an area where difficulties emerge.

Behavioral Difficulties

While many internalizing problems arise because of sexual abuse, such as depression and anxiety, which can lead to other concerns (i.e., medical), externalizing problems, such as behavioral disorders, may develop. There may be differences in the type of behavioral difficulties noted depending on the age of the child. Research conducted by Wilgosh (1993) suggested younger children tended to display aggressive or regressive behaviors whereas research conducted by McCarthy (2001) suggested older children exhibited more behavioral difficulties at school as well as risky behaviors such as substance abuse and nonsuicidal self-injury. Generally speaking, symptoms such as increased anxiety and behavioral difficulties, including aggression towards others and property, may be associated with reactions to trauma (Ryan, 1994; Russell & Shah, 2003).

Revictimization

Survivors of sexual abuse are at increased risk for suffering from additional sexual assault, known as revictimization. Revictimization is especially prominent when engaging in risky behaviors, such as drinking alcohol or abusing substances. Survivors of adolescent sexual abuse are more likely to engage in risky sexual behaviors and are at an increased risk for these behaviors as older adolescents or young adults (Testa, Hoffman, & Livingston, 2010). Examples of sexually risky behaviors include having unprotected sex or having multiple partners. Thus, they become more vulnerable to revictimization. The same pattern is true of alcohol consumption (Testa, Hoffman & Livingston, 2010).

Chances of revictimization in adolescence or adulthood also increase if the initial abuse was perpetrated by a trusted individual, indicating a high level of betrayal for the survivor (Gobin & Freyd, 2009). This means that survivors who knew and trusted their perpetrators are at a higher risk of experiencing a future sexual assault. This cycle of revictimization may be linked to an inability to correctly identify specific partner betrayal later in development (Gobin & Freyd, 2009). Meaning, that survivors who were abused by trusted individuals may have difficulty noticing and reacting to betrayal in future relationships. Individuals within the developmentally disabled population may be at increased risk for victimization and revictimization due to potentially poorer social skills, less social connections, increased isolation, as well as increased susceptibility to manipulation or threats if cognitive impairments are present.

Intimate Relationships

Survivors of sexual abuse often demonstrate decreased sexual libido (WHO, 2002) or issues with later sexual functioning. Feiring, Simon, and Cleland (2009) studied the relationship between childhood or adolescent sexual abuse and adult romantic relationships. Results from the study revealed that stigmatization, posttraumatic symptoms (e.g., hyperarousal, avoidance) and depressive symptoms (e.g., sad mood, poor sleep) in adult survivors were influential in creating and maintaining sexual difficulties in adult romantic relationships. Adult survivors who suffer from consequences associated with the abuse are more likely to have sexual difficulties in their intimate relationships. Stigmatization was defined as self-blame for the abuse and shame regarding the abuse. Furthermore, the level of stigmatization felt was predictive of the level of sexual difficulties, meaning that the more the survivor blamed themselves for the abuse the higher the chance was that they would have sexual difficulties in their relationships. Sexual difficulties may include inability or difficulties related to sexual arousal, orgasm, and sexual performance. Survivors may also exhibit a fear of appropriate sexual relations and have low libido, or the desire to engage in sexual acts. Besides sexual functioning, other aspects of intimate relationships are affected in survivors of abuse. Lower relationship satisfaction is often found and, unfortunately, survivors are also at increased risk for being in unhealthy, unsafe relationships (Testa, VanZile-Thomsen, & Livingston, 2005). Additionally, childhood sexual abuse survivors who experienced significant depressive symptoms (e.g., sadness, fatigue, and decreased appetite) as well as posttraumatic symptoms (e.g., flashbacks, exaggerated startle response, and emotional numbness) are more likely to experience dating aggression. Therefore, the more psychiatric symptoms (e.g., depression and PTSD) a survivor experiences due to abuse history, the more likely the survivor is to experience domestic violence, sexual aggression, and generally unhealthy intimate relationships (Feiring, Simon, & Cleland, 2009).

General Protective Factors

Protective factors also exist to either prohibit abuse or help the individual cope and heal from abuse. Such factors include solid support systems, psychological care, and educational programs (WHO, 2002). Therapy and intervention programs can help a survivor of abuse work through consequences of the assault and provide empowerment. Caring social supports, such as family members and friends, can create a loving safe environment for the survivor. Prevention programs aim to educate people on risk factors and consequences of abuse, as well as work to empower individuals and help to create a safe environment free from abuse. Interventions focused on prevention will be discussed in subsequent chapters of this workbook.

Chapter 2

BRIEF OVERVIEW OF DEVELOPMENTAL DISABILITIES (DD)

As stated previously in the Introduction the term "developmental disability" applies to a wide variety of conditions with varying functioning levels and severity. This workbook is intended for individuals who are moderate or high functioning and the following information is meant as a brief overview of more common developmental disorders to increase understanding of assessment and treatment interventions discussed. Clinicians should consult with medical providers and other knowledgeable professionals as well as research any condition in which they intend to treat. Furthermore, clinicians must recognize if treating an individual is outside the scope of their professional practice and should refer that individual when appropriate.

Borderline Intellectual Functioning

Borderline intellectual functioning (BIF) is determined by intellectual testing. If the individual obtains an IQ (intelligent quotient) score of 70 to 85 during intelligence testing they are considered have borderline intellectual functioning. Cognitive and intellectual level should not be assumed based on the presence of a developmental disability but should be evaluated through a formal assessment

BIF is considered a mild cognitive impairment; however, individuals within this range of cognitive functioning generally do not qualify for specialized services as they are not considered to have an intellectual disability, such as mental retardation. Individuals within the borderline range of intellectual functioning often have academic difficulties, including struggles with learning and applying information. They may be concrete thinkers. These individuals are generally able to care for themselves and do not show serious adaptive functioning deficits. Social-emotional and behavioral difficulties may be present.

Down's Syndrome

Down's syndrome is a genetic disorder caused by a third copy of chromosome 21. It is often referred to as trisomy 21 and is associated with physical growth and maturation delays as well as specific facial features. A variety of other conditions may co-occur with Down's syndrome, including mental retardation, speech and language difficulties, sensory difficulties, emotional, and behavior problems. Clinicians should not assume that these conditions co-occur but should rely on professional evaluations and assessments. Medical concerns need to fully assessed and addressed as well. Adaptive functioning levels may vary greatly from individual to individual and should be considered and incorporated appropriately for each person. Family members may also require increased support and consultation with other providers are important considerations.

Cerebral Palsy (CP)

CP is a movement disorder where an individual has difficulty managing muscle movement. Etiology of this disorder is not always known but can occur due to prenatal toxins, infections, or injury while in utero as well as injury following birth. CP is classified by the area of body affected, for example, quadriplegia refers to impairment in all four limbs, as well as the type of movement difficulty the individuals suffers. There are a variety of conditions that may co-occur with CP including behavioral and attention disorders, anxiety, impaired cognitive functioning, and sensory difficulties. Clinicians must also consider any medical difficulties if the individual experienced a significant injury.

Nonverbal Learning Disorder (NVLD)

NVLD is considered a neurobehavioral disorder and is often classified as learning disorder, not otherwise specified. This disorder is often difficult to detect and is often misdiagnosed as an attention disorder or autistic spectrum disorder, although those disorders may co-occur with NVLD. Anxiety and mood difficulties are often present and should be assessed as well. The main areas of difficulty for individuals with NVLD include information processing, sensory functioning, social skills and may also include deficits related to motor coordination. These areas of concern need to be considered when designing and implementing therapeutic interventions to ensure optimal understanding and engagement within therapy services.

Autism Spectrum Disorder

The autism spectrum encompasses a wide range of severity and functioning levels. In the *Diagnostic and Statistical Manual* Fourth Edition Text Revision (*DSM-IV-TR*: American Psychiatric Association, 2000) Asperger's syndrome is defined an impairment in social interaction, restricted or stereotyped patterns of behavior, interest, and activities without a significant delay in language. Additional difficulties may include sensory dysregulation, underdeveloped motor skills, concrete thinking, and limited theory of mind. Asperger's syndrome is now classified as part of an autism spectrum disorder in the *Diagnostic and Statistical Manual* Fifth Edition (DSM 5: American Psychiatric Association, 2013).

Individuals on the autism spectrum who are considered high functioning may have an IQ of 70 or above, but have symptoms related to impairment in social interactions, communication, as well as restricted, repetitive, and stereotyped patterns of behaviors, interests, and activities. Moderate to low functioning individuals on the spectrum may have severe communication difficulties, such as limited to no verbal language, and significant deficits in social interaction and adaptive functioning.

Attention Deficit/Hyperactivity Disorder (ADHD)

ADHD is one of, if not the most, commonly researched and diagnosed childhood disorder. According to the *DSM 5* (American Psychiatric Association, 2013), symptoms include deficits in attention and/or hyperactivity as well as impulse control deficits appearing prior to age 12 in multiple settings. Subtypes include predominately inattentive, predominately hyperactive/impulsive, and a combined subtype. ADHD often co-occurs with behavioral, learning, mood and anxiety disorders. Clinicians providing treatment to individuals with ADHD who experienced sexual abuse should be aware that ADHD and trauma symptoms may look similar and be difficult, if possible at all, to differentiate. For example, daydreaming behaviors of an inattentive child look similar to dissociation related to trauma.

Fetal Alcohol Effects

Fetal alcohol syndrome is diagnosed when there is a specific pattern of physical and cognitive symptoms identified in a child who was exposed to alcohol while in utero. Fetal alcohol effects lie on a spectrum of disability and impairment. Fetal alcohol effects are considered less severe and are often seen as a subthreshold case of fetal alcohol syndrome. Comorbid conditions to assess for include lowered cognitive functioning, academic difficulties, and intellectual disabilities. Behavioral and social-emotional difficulties are often present and require intervention as well.

Additional Considerations

A variety of additional concerns and difficulties may co-occur with developmental disabilities due to medical, physical, and cognitive impairments. Sensory dysregulation, motor and coordination disorders, and feeding disorders are prevalent. Many individuals within the developmentally disabled population seek services from professionals in a variety of disciplines to address these concerns, such as occupational therapists. Clinicians should be informed of any condition present within an individual in treatment and consult with outside providers. This is especially true in trauma treatment as these conditions may impact the way in which the individual processes and manages the traumatizing experience as well as engages in treatment. For example, a child with a tactile dysfunction may need increased support and therapeutic interventions surrounding the physical aspects of sexual abuse. Clinicians can also consult with supervisors, colleagues, and professionals knowledgeable in these areas.

Chapter 3

ASSESSMENT AND TREATMENT GUIDELINES FOR CHILDREN, ADOLESCENTS, AND YOUNG ADULTS WITH DEVELOPMENTAL DISABILITIES WHO EXPERIENCED SEXUAL ABUSE

GENERAL GUIDELINES FOR TRAUMA-INFORMED ASSESSMENT WITH CHILDREN, ADOLESCENTS, AND YOUNG ADULTS WITH DEVELOPMENTAL DISABILITIES

Trauma treatment for sexual abuse, as all other treatments, should begin with a thorough evaluation period, including but not limited to clinical interviews or intakes. Children, adolescents, and young adults with a sexual abuse history present with complex histories and symptoms which can often be difficult to differentiate from other conditions. For example, a child with a significant trauma history may be inattentive at times and appear to dissociate with a blank stare. In this example, it is important to differentiate if these symptoms are related to an attention disorder, trauma disorder, a combination of both, or other factors. Thus, it is recommended that a thorough trauma assessment be completed for any individual entering trauma-informed treatment. This is especially true for individuals with developmental disabilities as they may communicate in different ways or experience or express trauma symptoms differently than their nondisabled peers.

Trauma assessments are not forensic evaluations. Forensic evaluations are generally meant to determine the details of the perpetration of sexual abuse. If this type of service is needed, individuals should be referred to a local child advocacy center that provides medical, legal, and forensic services prior to initiating trauma treatment. Additionally, clinicians are mandated reporters, meaning that they are legally obligated to report child abuse to the appropriate authorities. While each state differs in reporting procedures, each clinician must be aware and follow their state's reporting laws.

Trauma evaluations and/or assessments may or may not include more formal psychological testing. Psychological testing is typically conducted by a clinical psychologist, and then a formal report is created based on the testing results that provides a more comprehensive understanding of the person. However, clinicians that are thorough and focused can conduct a trauma evaluation that consists of several components. A full report may or may not arise from this process, however, when completed a trauma evaluation should help the clinician better understand the client and their conditions and diagnoses, treatment needs and goals, and generate recommendations and referrals to other providers if needed. Trauma assessments should consider any present mental health diagnoses, intellectual ability, medical conditions, psychosocial stressors, and current functioning level. It is also important to incorporate family system dynamics and the child's inherent strengths and resources into case conceptualization and treatment planning to best treat the individual. Often individuals with developmental disabilities are viewed with deficits in mind rather than strengths and wellness factors, so this component is especially important.

A variety of disorders may be seen in this population. Disorders such as Cerebral Palsy, Down Syndrome, Autistic Spectrum Disorders, Attention Deficit/Hyperactivity Disorder (ADHD), Nonverbal Learning Disorder, and Fetal Alcohol Syndrome or Effects may be seen. Additionally, motor, communication, sensory, and feeding problems are frequent. These disorders each lie on a wide spectrum of functioning level and severity, thus it is important to tailor treatment to the needs of the individual. Therapists need to be aware of any biases in working with these populations as well as concerns related to providing treatment. Some if not most children with developmental disabilities require additional services, such as occupational therapy, speech therapy, or individual counseling that incorporates caregivers, psychiatrists, medication treatment services, and educational specialists at their school. Take a careful history of their past services, and if they were considered helpful or not. If these services are not already in place prior to trauma-informed treatment, therapists should make appropriate referrals for additional services. Trauma-informed treatment will not be as effective if an individual is not receiving all needed services. Be aware that while schools may provide some services, it can be extremely helpful or necessary to have independent providers outside the school system to evaluate and provide these additional services. Many times, families rely on schools to diagnose and treat their children without other objective external providers giving alternate perspectives and guidance. Also, schools may not be as open and direct to suggest families contact other providers. Sometimes caregivers and parents may not be aware of how other providers can enhance the care of individuals with developmental disabilities. Please refer to Chapter 8 for additional information on a variety of adjunct services children with developmental disabilities may require.

When diagnosing individuals who experienced trauma therapists should consider *DSM* 5 trauma and stress-related diagnoses, such as Posttraumatic Stress Disorder (PTSD), Acute Stress Disorder, Adjustment Disorder with Anxiety, Dissociative Disorder, Anxiety Disorder Unspecified, Attachment Disorders, and T and Z codes for abuse and neglect (*DSM* 5: American Psychiatric Association, 2013). Children, adolescents, and young adults with developmental disabilities may exhibit trauma related symptoms in an idiosyncratic way, such as a child on the autistic spectrum with limited communication. Following a trauma this child may engage in more hand-flapping or increased self-stimulation which would not be apparent in a child without a developmental disability.

Additional diagnoses, such as behavioral disorders, may be applicable. Individuals with developmental disabilities may enter treatment with a history of diagnoses or behavioral symptoms which were exacerbated by sexual abuse. Each therapist must carefully assess the history of presenting symptoms, differential diagnoses, and comorbidity issues. To obtain comprehensive information about behavioral functioning, caregivers and/or persons familiar with the individual should be included in the assessment process.

Children with developmental disabilities may have a variety of medical conditions or issues that may impact their social-emotional or relational functioning as well as their physical health. Recommendations because of a trauma assessment should be relevant to diagnoses and other treatment needs, such as occupational therapy services for sensory integration difficulties. Remember that individuals with developmental disabilities who are not receiving adequate or appropriate services will be less likely to fully participate and benefit from trauma-informed treatment.

During this initial evaluation phase consider the variety of psychosocial stressors present in the child or adolescent. It is important to assess for current safety level, especially given the dependency on caregivers, as well as prior traumas. Consider legal, medical, and environmental stressors. Evaluators are likely to spend a higher amount of time in this area as children with developmental disabilities often have various stressors unique to their condition, such as self-care issues. Symptoms that cause difficulty but do not meet clear or more apparent criteria for a diagnosis should also be reviewed; examples may include severe temper tantrums or head-banging.

Evaluators must integrate previous psychological evaluations, assessment, and reports from a variety of disciplines into their assessment, case conceptualization, and treatment planning for appropriate trauma-informed treatment for children, adolescents, and young adults with developmental disabilities. A current cognitive assessment, which helps to clarify intelligence level and other cognitive functions of an individual, is crucial to inform the clinician of the individual's level of functioning so the clinician can best tailor treatment to match accordingly.

As part of the assessment process, evaluators must conduct comprehensive clinical diagnostic interviews, which will last several sessions. Clinicians who proceed to treatment quickly and do not take adequate time during this important initial evaluation phase often miss critical aspects to address in treatment and can be less effective in therapy. Evaluators must meet with the caregivers and the child, adolescent, or young adult. It is important to meet with the caregiver(s) alone and the child/adolescent alone for at least a portion or entire full session of the initial sessions during the assessment process. Explain to the caregivers, as well as the child, adolescent, or young adult, why you are doing this, the limits of confidentiality, and obtain informed consent. Clinicians should use language that is developmentally-appropriate to explain these concepts to the child, adolescent, or young adult. Reasons for conducting a separate interview include making each individual feel more comfortable in reviewing certain aspects of the trauma or background information as well as reducing possible anxiety in revealing background information unknown to the other. Also, children, adolescents, and even young adults may react differently when in the presence of a caregiver. Be aware that some individuals may struggle to accurately identify emotions, behaviors, or may have limited self-awareness. Additionally, due to the inherited aspect of some developmental disabilities, some caregivers with impairments may struggle with similar issues as their children, such as social relatedness, or dependency issues. As stated previously, trauma assessments are not forensic interviews or evaluations and individuals should be referred to child advocacy centers for forensic concerns and legal issues, as child sexual abuse is a crime.

Obtaining teacher reports can be helpful as well as obtaining reports from other important individuals. Examples of other individuals may include an occupational therapist the child sees for treatment several times a week. First, make sure to obtain a signed release of information to speak with any outside provider or important person connected to the individual. For children, adolescents, and young adults with developmental disabilities, it may be helpful to obtain behavioral observations, teacher reports, or collaborate via phone with special education teachers, occupational therapists, or other providers. Information regarding the child's behaviors or symptoms is the most accurate when a variety of settings are considered.

Evaluators should utilize specific trauma measures in assessing the level of trauma symptoms or impact of the trauma, if any, on the child's diagnoses and level of functioning. Evaluators should consider the individual's reading level and administer appropriate measures. Evaluators need be aware of the ways data are interpreted as elevations on particular scales may be associated with certain developmental disability symptoms, trauma symptoms, or a combination of both. Additionally, individuals may require additional assistance in completing self-report measures, such as the examiner reading the question and the individual verbally responding or the evaluator asking the individual to paraphrase what was said to ensure understanding. Other visual aids may be required as well for individual responses such as a visual response sheet. Make note and discuss any accommodations made during assessment as it may influence the validity of test results. Note any confounding variables that may alter the validity and reliability of the measure, such as speech, language, or motor difficulties. Furthermore, make sure to choose instruments that are appropriate to the individual's cognitive and developmental level as well as chronological age.

Evaluators may determine that a neuropsychological or neurodevelopmental assessment needed prior to a trauma assessment as some individuals may not have previous or recent evaluations assessing levels of functioning related to their developmental disability, or if diagnoses are difficult to differentiate. Evaluators may determine that comprehensive psychological testing is warranted as well. The need for a proper diagnosis prior to trauma treatment is crucial in the ability to modify trauma treatment appropriately for this population.

General Guidelines for Trauma-Informed Treatment with Children, Adolescents, and Young Adults with Developmental Disabilities

Children, adolescents, and young adults with developmental disabilities are more likely to experience sexual abuse in comparison to their peers making prevention and safety skills training paramount in trauma-informed treatment. There is currently no specific evidenced-based treatment or gold standard to utilize for children, adolescents, and young adults with developmental disabilities who have experienced child sexual abuse. Therefore, current best practice is to utilize evidenced-based trauma treatments with accommodations and special considerations for individuals with developmental disabilities. Each individual will have unique needs, thus each and any treatment approach must incorporate the symptoms, behaviors, challenges, and strengths the individual demonstrates as well as be appropriate for the individual's developmental level, cognitive level, and social-emotional/relational functioning.

Trauma treatment with this population is also unique in that auxiliary treatments are likely needed outside of trauma treatment to best regulate the child, adolescent, or young adult and address all relevant needs. One example includes occupational therapy services for a child with motor or sensory issues.

It is paramount that the clinician incorporates the family system into treatment to not only enhance the individual treatment but also provide support, relevant psychosocial skills, and services to that system. For example, the parent or caregiver may need behavioral management techniques to manage disruptive behaviors at home, or siblings may be experiencing less attention due to the special needs of a sibling with developmental disabilities thus requiring more intervention or guidance. The clinician should utilize a collaborative framework with parents or caregivers to address these issues. The clinician should engage in a collaborative relationship with all outside treatment providers as well.

Trauma treatment should emphasize psychoeducation as well as the development of appropriate safety skills to prevent future victimization. Specific psychoeducation and safety skills that are important to focus on for this population include the ability to recognize inappropriate behaviors of others as well as ways to report inappropriate behaviors to trusted adults. Providers should be aware that children, adolescents, and young adults with developmental disabilities already face prejudice regarding sexuality or societal views portraying them as helpless or asexual or insensitive to pain (i.e., the perception being that because of limited reasoning abilities, these children do not suffer as they do not understand what has happened to them). Thus, appropriate psychoeducation regarding healthy and normal sexuality and sexual behaviors is important for the both the child and the caregivers. Clinicians can distribute appropriate handouts to caregivers as well as age-appropriate materials that children, adolescents, and young adults can understand during sessions.

While providing prevention skills to both children and caregivers is important, caregivers of children, adolescents, or young adults with developmental disabilities may be overprotective or infantilize these individuals, especially after a traumatic event. It is always important to understand the family members' reactions to the traumatic event(s) and incorporate the family system into treatment. The use of social stories, role-plays, as well as expressive therapies can be helpful in safety skill training and can provide the survivor with an adaptive verbal script or behavioral repertoire to use in difficult situations, especially if the individual struggles with communication difficulties or has limited social skills.

It is important for clinicians to recognize that children, adolescents, and young adults with developmental disabilities may struggle to understand and manage social situations. A social skills treatment component or social skills group is essential to helping the child, adolescents, or young adult understand appropriate boundaries and behaviors between adults and children or peers. Take into account that the survivor may not be aware that the abusive relationship was maladaptive and may struggle to understand adaptive and appropriate social boundaries and relationships.

In treatment, clinicians should consider the possibility of increased difficulty for children, adolescents, and young adults with developmental disabilities to understand and use abstract ideas or concepts. Treatment interventions and psychoeducation need to be as concrete as possible. Additionally, try to keep a consistent structure to your treatment as disruptions or changes in routines may be dysregulating for this population. It may be helpful to utilize pre-teaching to reduce any anxiety the individual may experience regarding treatment. Examples of pre-teaching may include reviewing the agenda for the session at the beginning of the session. Additionally, visual aids/schedules may be helpful. Along with visual aids, consider the individual's communication style and preference. A written trauma narrative may not be appropriate for a child, adolescent, or young adult with a communication difficulty; however, alternate ways in to process trauma are just as valid. Special recommendations of speech therapists, occupational therapists, or teachers should be generalized to treatment sessions as well. Take into consideration any special accommodations provided at school and how to integrate these accommodations into therapy, as appropriate.

Be aware of the level of sensory stimuli in your office. Bright lights or noises from other offices may be dysregulating and may create an uncomfortable environment for individuals with developmental disabilities which will create difficulty in trauma treatment. Make sure to consider the impact of the sensory experience of sexual abuse on a child, adolescent, or young adult. For example, children with tactile defensiveness may experience different aspects of the abuse as traumatic over other aspects, such as the experience of a sense of betrayal. Consider and process the "rule-breaking" behavior of sexual abuse. Individuals who are concrete thinkers or engage in rule-governed behavior may struggle to understand the perpetrator's abusive behavior, especially if the perpetrator utilized verbal threats, e.g., to harm others if they were to tell, or manipulated the child, adolescent, or young adult due to a concrete thinking style. Furthermore, individuals with greater dependency needs have a higher reliance on others to meet their needs, thus when children, adolescents, or young adults with developmental disabilities are abused by a trusted caregiver, it can lead to increased feelings of isolation, low self-esteem, and difficulties with affect regulation.

Finally, treatment effectiveness will increase when the clinician takes into account the developmental tasks and milestones the individual is trying to master and anticipate future tasks/milestones for relapse prevention. For example, puberty can be a developmental time that exacerbates trauma related symptoms. In this example, relapse prevention may consist of psychoeducation regarding puberty, trauma triggers, and healthy relationships as well as the development and review of adaptive coping skills to utilize during this developmental period. And of course, throughout treatment, always utilize the individual's strengths, be empathic, and be hopeful.

Chapter 4

TRAUMA TREATMENT MODELS AND PREPARING FOR TRAUMA TREATMENT

Trauma treatment for sexual abuse and maltreatment can include individual, family, and group modalities. While there are numerous therapies and treatments to address sexual abuse, there are a number of evidenced-based or highly-supported treatments that are important to review. These trauma treatments are gold standards in the trauma field. It is important to note that to best understand and accommodate children, adolescents, and young adults with developmental disabilities and a history of sexual abuse, it is important to understand current best practices to make appropriate accommodations. Suggestions for accommodations for individuals with developmental disabilities were provided in the previous chapter and can be applied to the treatments discussed below. Please note that this chapter is meant to provide a brief overview of two trauma treatment models, please see applicable resources including the appropriate treatment manual for each model for the most comprehensive information.

Trauma-Focused Cognitive-Behavioral Treatment (TF-CBT)

Trauma-Focused Cognitive-Behavioral Treatment (TF-CBT), developed by Cohen, Deblinger, and Mannarino (2006) is an empirically-based treatment for children experiencing trauma symptoms (Cohen, Mannarino, & Deblinger, 2006). TF-CBT is appropriate to use for children, adolescents, and young adults exposed to trauma and are experiencing either behavioral, cognitive, or affective trauma symptoms. Treatment modalities utilized within TF-CBT include individual and joint therapy sessions with the child and caregiver. Developing a positive therapeutic relationship is crucial in TF-CBT. Each session is focused and structured to provide appropriate psychoeducation, skill development, and a safe environment for the individual.

Cohen, Deblinger, and Mannarino (2006) developed the acronym PRACTICE to summarize the following TF-CBT treatment components: psychoeducation and parenting component, relaxation techniques, affective regulation, cognitive coping skills, trauma narrative, in-vivo exposure, conjoint sessions with caregiver and child, and enhancing future safety. Clinicians can refer to http://tfcbt.musc.edu/ to access the TF-CBT training online and to become more familiar with each treatment component.

Integrative Treatment of Complex Trauma (ITCT)

Integrative Treatment of Complex Trauma (ITCT) is an empirically-validated and component-based treatment for traumatized children, adolescents, young adults, and families developed by Drs. John N. Briere and Cheryl B. Lanktree. Two versions of ITCT were developed and include a child model (ITCT-C; Lanktree & Briere, 2008) for children between the ages of 8-12 and an adolescent model (ITCT-A; Briere & Lanktree, 2012) for individuals between the ages of 13-21. ITCT is generally utilized for survivors of chronic or complex trauma. Complex trauma occurs when a child or adolescent is exposed to different types of trauma or had multiple exposures to one type of trauma, such as sexual abuse.

ITCT (Briere & Lanktree, 2012) is an assessment-focused intervention meaning that the clinician regularly assesses the individual at the beginning and throughout the course of treatment to determine level and severity of symptoms, problem areas, as well as assesses for treatment progress. Regular assessment allows the clinician to treat the most current and relevant concerns presented by the client and is flexible to address the numerous and varied needs of individuals who experienced chronic or complex traumas. Examples of possible symptoms include attachment difficulties, social deficits, acting out behaviors, and affective dysregulation. Doctors Briere and Lanktree (2012) encourage advocacy as a part of treatment, specifically, collaboration and coordination with multiple community agencies and systems as needed. And, of course, interventions are developmentally and culturally appropriate, adapted for the community and setting.

Furthermore, Doctors Briere and Lanktree (2012) developed a Problems-to-Component Grid (PCG) to aide clinicians in identifying problem areas and related ITCT treatment components to address the problem area. There are numerous treatment components included in ITCT and include relationship building and support, safety, psychoeducation, distress reduction and affect regulation, cognitive processing, trigger identification, exposure, relational processing, and identity interventions (Briere & Lanktree, 2012). Modalities of ITCT include individual therapy, family therapy, caregiver support, and possible group sessions.

Resources

Please see the Appendix for additional resources for trauma treatment, additional resources specific to individuals with developmental disabilities, and for general resources.

Preparing for Trauma Treatment

There are several important issues to consider as a clinician prior to the initiation of trauma-focused therapy services with individuals with developmental disabilities. While every clinician should consider and manage an appropriate therapeutic space to create a sense of safety and security, children, adolescents, and young adults with developmental disabilities tend to require additional accommodations.

Clinicians should be aware and manage the level of sensory input within their space, such as the type and intensity of lighting. Some children may have sensory processing and/or integration difficulties or simply be more sensitive to sensory input in comparison to children in the general population. If the sensory input within the therapeutic space is disruptive to the child, then they will not be fully available to engage in the therapeutic process and may become dysregulated in your office.

Furthermore, clinicians need to consider the layout of a therapeutic space and the ease of access to the space for the individual in treatment. Many individuals with developmental disabilities have medical concerns or require medical interventions, such as the use of a wheelchair or require additional space or a sensory area for motor or sensory concerns. If the therapeutic space cannot accommodate the specific needs of the individual, trauma treatment will not be effective.

Additionally, clinicians should be aware of appropriate boundaries within the therapeutic space. Many children within this specialized population struggle with appropriate social skills and behaviors, thus they may engage in inappropriate behaviors such as attempting to sit on the clinician's lap or excessively hugging the clinician. Part of treatment is to provide psychoeducation and model appropriate behaviors, however, clinicians should determine a repertoire of clinical interventions to utilize in order to maintain appropriate boundaries. Examples may include the use of hula-hoop to visually illustrate personal space or redirection of inappropriate social behavior. Clinicians should be aware that inappropriate or inadequate social behaviors may also be a result of or contributing factor to a history of abuse and thus an integral part of trauma treatment.

Clinicians can set up a particular structure or agenda to session as well to help ease the child in and out of the therapeutic space, as transition times may be difficult for some of the children in this population. Visual aids and schedules may be helpful in creating this structure and boundaries in therapy.

Lastly, therapeutic rapport can begin to be built prior to the first session, specifically with caregivers. Any contact a clinician has with the child and/or the family prior to the initiation of services, e.g., phone contact to discuss services or schedule an intake session, is considered part of therapeutic rapport. Clinicians should utilize appropriate therapeutic skills in these contacts, such as active and/or reflective listening and empathic statements.

Therapeutic rapport continues throughout the treatment process, especially in the beginning of services, however, disruptions or breaks in rapport can occur as treatment progresses. Additionally, children and adolescents with a history of sexual abuse may require additional time, support, and relational building to feel comfortable in treatment. Adolescents and young adults with developmental disabilities and a history of abuse may require additional support in treatment to feel accepted by the clinician due to the rejection they can experience from others as a person with a disability.

Prior to treatment clinicians must familiarize themselves with the child's unique medical needs and/or developmental condition, which may require outside consultation or further research. If a clinician is unable to accommodate or appropriately treat a child, an appropriate referral list should be on hand. Additionally, clinicians can spend time reviewing previous evaluations and records prior to treatment to get a better sense of the child's abilities and functioning levels in a variety of domains.

Chapter 5

TRAUMA TREATMENT WITH CHILDREN, ADOLESCENTS, AND YOUNG ADULTS WITH DEVELOPMENTAL DISABILITIES (TT-CAYDD)

Children, adolescents, and young adults with developmental disabilities that experienced sexual abuse have a right to evidenced-based treatments and thus, the gold standard for these individuals should incorporate best practices in the trauma field. The model presented in this workbook, TT-CAYDD, was created by incorporating different trauma treatment model components while integrating perspectives and approaches sensitive to individuals with developmental disabilities. Accommodations for each child are needed to best suit their needs and provide the most appropriate and effective treatment. While each child has unique strengths and difficulties, children, adolescents, and young adults with developmental disabilities may have specific factors to consider in treatment. Brief information related to different modules we consider to appropriately address these treatment factors is included in this chapter. TT-CAYDD includes psychoeducation, affect regulation (identification and modulation), coping skill acquisition, self-awareness and mindfulness, relational and social skills, sex education/healthy relationships/body awareness, addressing sexual behavior problems (if applicable), safety skill training, and a trauma narrative. The following chapters will provide a more detailed description and information related to each module for children, adolescents, and young adults with developmental disabilities who are survivors of sexual abuse.

Psychoeducation

Psychoeducation is a core component of any treatment modality. It is generally utilized most heavily during the beginning stages of treatment, however, psychoeducation should occur throughout the treatment process. Psychoeducation can be understood as when the therapist provides important information to the child, adolescent, or young adult and caregivers regarding mental health issues, such as diagnoses, symptom presentation, and effects of trauma. Therapists should take special caution to educate individuals and caregivers in a way that they can understand fully. Psychoeducation regarding therapy, the role of the therapist, trauma, and common trauma reactions are an essential focus during the initial phase of therapy. Any special considerations regarding the child's developmental disability and if applicable, the relationship between the child's developmental disability and the trauma should be reviewed. An example may be a child with communication difficulties being more susceptible to sexual abuse due to the perpetrator's view that the child cannot report the abuse. Alternative forms of communicating inappropriate behaviors should be incorporated into safety planning. Psychoeducation should be incorporated into other modules of treatment as well. For example, in safety skill training it is important for the therapist to provide developmentally-appropriate information on how to stay safe and the importance for utilizing safety skills.

Affect Regulation (Identification and Modulation)

Affect regulation consists of several different components, specifically, affect identification and affect modulation. Affect identification refers to the child's ability to correctly identify a variety of emotions in themselves as well as others. This should include identifying physiological reactions to emotions, i.e., stomachache due to anxiety, as well as triggers to emotions. Children and young adults should be able to identify facial expressions and body language of others in identifying emotions. Affect identification can be a hard task for survivors of trauma. Some individuals may engage in numbing or avoidance behaviors, and thus be resistant to identifying and connecting with their own internal experiences. Additionally, children with certain developmental disabilities, such as children who are diagnosed on the autistic spectrum, may inherently struggle with affect regulation. Thus, this component of treatment is crucial, may comprise a large portion of treatment, and needs to be individualized to each child's social-emotional level of functioning and understanding. Affect regulation also consists of affect modulation. Affect modulation refers to the child's ability to manage the level of intensity of an emotion, which is often accomplished using adaptive coping skills.

Cognitive

A cognitive component of trauma treatment is important to aid the child, adolescent, or young adult in identifying any maladaptive thoughts about themselves, others/the world, and the future that may be distorted following sexual abuse. This may be challenging for individuals within the developmentally disabled population due to the level of type of developmental disability present as metacognition and abstract thinking may be difficult for individuals with more concrete thinking styles. Many survivors of sexual abuse, especially when abuse is committed by trusted caregiver, experience a shift in the ways they may think about themselves and others, such that they may feel as if they are to blame, that the world is an unsafe place, and that they are inherently bad. Helping a child or adolescent identify maladaptive thoughts or cognitive distortions as well as reframe maladaptive thoughts can improve a child's self-esteem as well as increase his or her level of understanding of the incident so they can further process the trauma. Additionally, a healthy alteration in cognitive processing will positively impact the individual's emotional functioning and lessen any disruptive behaviors resulting from the trauma. Due to the wide range of cognitive functioning a child with a developmental disability may experience, special accommodations must be made; for example, utilizing concrete rather than abstract strategies would be important for a child or adolescent on the autistic spectrum. Some individuals may have slower processing speed but enhanced verbal abilities or borderline intellectual functioning. To be most effective, therapy interventions should match individuals' strengths as well as support their weaknesses. Again, visual aids and concrete examples may be helpful. The use of bibliotherapy, or social stories, may be particularly influential during this module of treatment. Social stories are narratives created by the therapist which aim to teach a child adaptive skills in a particular situation.

Coping Skills

Coping skills can be defined as the intentional use of a variety of techniques to lessen distress. For a child, adolescent, or young adult to utilize healthy coping skills, they must first be able to identify when distress. Once able to do so, an individual can engage in various behaviors to gain a sense of control over his or her affective experience and lessen distress. Many survivors of trauma will naturally engage in a variety of coping skills in an attempt to reduce distress, however, not all of these coping strategies are healthy. For example, many survivors of child sexual abuse utilize nonsuicidal self-injury or abuse substances as a coping mechanism. Thus, it is important for therapists to not only teach and promote healthy coping skills during this phase of treatment, such as deep breathing, relaxation exercises, or the use of expressive modalities but accurately assess for any coping mechanisms the child may be already utilizing. These coping mechanisms may be more difficult to detect because of lower levels of self-awareness and/ or communication difficulties. One example may be increased self-stimulation behavior of a child on the autistic spectrum. Therapists should collaborate with any auxiliary services, such as an occupational therapist, in identifying or creating particular behaviors or routines specific to the child that will help him or her regulate distress levels. These can then be incorporated into the trauma treatment.

Self-Awareness and Mindfulness

Mindfulness can be a powerful component to trauma treatment to help increase a child, adolescent or young adult's self-awareness. Often survivors of trauma feel disconnected from or threatened by their emotions, bodies, and sense of self. Mindfulness is a basic practice that can help the individual reconnect with themselves as well practice increased understanding and integration of their experiences. Mindfulness refers to the intentional practice of bringing focus to an aspect of the self, such as breathing, in the present moment with complete acceptance of the experience and without judgment. Mindfulness can act as a healthy coping skill when distressed. Individuals with developmental disabilities may struggle to bring a focused attention to a specific behavior, thought, or part of their body depending on their level of cognitive functioning and ability to sustain focus as well as any physical or medical issues connected to their diagnoses. For example, an individual with cerebral palsy may struggle to bring attention to their breath if they are focused on the rigidity or spasm of muscles. However, mindfulness practices have been developed and are available for all developmental levels.

Mindfulness exercises can be broken down into a variety of steps for ease of use. Clinicians can role model and practice mindfulness with clients in session with the use of an audio recording to direct a mindfulness exercise. Additionally, a simple exercise such as eating a raisin can serve as a mindfulness intervention by bringing awareness and focused attention to aspects of the raisin and of eating that are generally ignored. Include caregivers in developing this skill as they can help the individual practice at home.

Social Skills/Healthy Relationships

Sexual abuse is viewed as an interpersonal trauma, meaning that the nature of the abuse impacts the way in which the individual subsequently relates or views others. This is especially true when the abuse is perpetrated by a family member or trusted adult. For a child, sexual abuse, apart from many other consequences, can be extremely confusing. The level of confusion and betrayal experienced by the child as well as the impact on their subsequent relational functioning can vary depending on the circumstances of the abuse (i.e., perpetrator) as well as the child's cognitive, developmental, and socio-emotional level. Many children with developmental disabilities may have poor social skills or relational functioning prior to abuse, which may make them targets for perpetrators. With a poor or limited understanding of appropriate relational functioning, these children may be easily manipulated by perpetrators. Thus, incorporating a relational/social skills component is important to trauma treatment to develop adaptive skills and knowledge as to what constitutes appropriate interactions, reducing a child's self-blame or self-assigned level of responsibility to their behaviors, and prevents future victimization as well as inappropriate sexual behaviors with others.

Sexuality and Sexual Behavior Problems

During puberty, preadolescents, adolescents, and young adults with developmental disabilities may exhibit many challenging behaviors. Preadolescents, adolescents, and young adults with DD experience hormonal changes and sexual curiosity during this time just as preadolescents and adolescents without DD experience them. One major difference though, is that individuals with DD experience these changes in addition to possible communication, socialization, and behavior problems. It is important for parents, caregivers, and professionals to recognize that it is common for individuals with DD to display challenging sexual behaviors (Van Bourgondien, Reichle, & Palmer, 1997). It is then important to understand the context in which the sexual behaviors occur to understand if the sexual behaviors are unhealthy or concerning and if so, the best matched intervention to address them. Most parents and caregivers of preadolescents, adolescents, and young adults with DD experience the challenge of teaching their preadolescents, adolescents, and young adults to behave in an appropriate sexual manner. When preadolescents, adolescents, and young adults are exhibiting typical and healthy sexual behaviors but in a socially inappropriate way, they usually respond well to adult redirection. However, preadolescents, adolescents, and young adults with DD may take longer to respond to adult intervention and they may require repeated redirection. Preadolescents, adolescents, and young adults exhibiting healthy sexual behavior typically show embarrassment, and rarely show more negative emotions such as shame or anxiety.

Preadolescents, adolescents, and young adults who are exhibiting repeated sexual behaviors despite repeated redirection by adults and/or their sexual behaviors are concerning or seem unhealthy, typically show feelings of shame and anxiety and they may require a more serious intervention. This may involve an assessment by a qualified professional to clarify the seriousness of the sexual behaviors and specialized therapy services delivered by a qualified professional may follow. Interventions that use simple and concrete behavior management principles that focus on specific rules and behavior intervention are most commonly used with children and adolescents with DD who are exhibiting unhealthy and concerning sexual behaviors. This is because children and adolescents with DD tend to have difficulty understanding more advanced or abstract concepts, so a more directive, experienced-based approach tends to work better. Examples of interventions could be psychoeducation, bibliotherapy, role-playing, practicing, and positive and negative reinforcement.

Sexual Behavior Problems

This component of treatment is only applicable in a minority of cases as not all children, adolescents, or young adults who experience sexual abuse go on to have sexual behavior problems, also known as sexual touching problems. Additionally, children, adolescents, or young adults with moderate to severe sexual behavior problems should be referred to specific sexual-behavior problem therapy. Some children without an abuse history do engage in sexually inappropriate behaviors, alone or with other children, due to impulsivity, lack of education or knowledge on appropriate sexual boundaries, social difficulties, or other difficulties. For example, children with developmental disabilities may engage in an increase in sexual self-stimulating behavior when distressed or as they enter puberty. Of course, safety is always a primary concern. If a child is engaging in sexual behaviors, such as behaviors with other children, younger children, or using coercion it may be appropriate to refocus treatment on specific sexual behavior problem therapy to target the sexual behavior problems. However, depending on the context of the behaviors, milder or self-directed behaviors (e.g., excessive masturbation) may be managed in trauma treatment. The first step is always creating an appropriate safety plan for that child, as inappropriate sexual behaviors can harm another child as well as put the child at increased risk for victimization. Psychoeducation, affect regulation, and the development of adaptive coping skills are important in decreasing inappropriate sexual behaviors.

Sex Education/Body Awareness

Individuals with developmental disabilities are often stigmatized as asexual beings, which is not true. However, because of this prejudice, many individuals with developmental disabilities are given even less, if any, sex education or information about their bodies. Thus, children with developmental disabilities are often targeted by perpetrators. Appropriate sex education and information about body awareness, puberty, and healthy sexual relationships is important for these individuals to develop a healthy concept of intimate relationships and sexuality. Children in this population may relate to their bodies in different ways than the general population depending on their physical state and medical needs. Developing an appropriate level of body esteem, or relating positively to one's body, is an important part of self-esteem that is often negatively impacted by abuse. A healthy level of body esteem can be developed during this module.

Safety Skill Training

Providing psychoeducation and skills related to safety is an important component of trauma treatment to reduce the risk of future victimization. Children who experience sexual abuse, especially by a trusted adult, may struggle to feel safe and engage in behaviors that put them at higher risk. Furthermore, children and adolescents with developmental disabilities may struggle to understand or engage in appropriate safety skills given their specific difficulties, i.e., social skill deficits. Individuals are also at higher risk of victimization due to possible communication difficulties or dependence on adult caregivers. Simple steps to increase safety may create a monumental impact. Visual aids as well as social stories are helpful in providing psychoeducation and skills related to safety training as well as provide practice for a child to utilize those skills. Repetition, rehearsal, and reminders can be necessary to teach safety skill.

Trauma Story

A trauma story is widely used in trauma-focused treatment and can act as an exposure technique as well as provide opportunities for an individual to further integrate and process their trauma. A trauma story can take many forms such as written, verbal, or art, however, no matter the form the purpose is for the child to "tell their story." The level of detail in a trauma story may vary although there are several important components to consider such as including thoughts, feelings, and events relevant to the abuse as well as creating a beginning, middle, and end to the narrative. A child may choose to start their story at any point in time they wish and can include hopes and plans for the future as the end of their story. Children with chronic or complex abuse histories can choose a specific incidence of abuse in which they want to feel better.

The trauma story is presented when a child has sufficient knowledge regarding trauma and demonstrates effective coping skills, as this module in treatment has the potential to increase disruptive behaviors or trigger anxiety symptoms. Caregivers are an important part of this module as the goal is for them to eventually witness and support their child's story. Some children may need these sessions to be highly structured and include a transition in and out of session. The therapist should help the child process thoughts and feelings associated with writing and expressing their trauma story.

Chapter 6

CAREGIVERS

DEFINE CAREGIVER ROLE: ADVOCATE, LIAISON, COLLABORATOR

The term caregiver denotes a variety of roles an adult may assume in a child's life. Caregivers are adult individuals who assume the responsibility for and care for a child, adolescent, or young adult. Caregivers often provide emotional and financial support and provide for the basic needs of a child, i.e., housing and food. Caregivers include but are not limited to biological, foster, or adoptive parents, grandparents, family members, babysitters, nannies, and caretakers who provide for an individual's needs. This may include employees of residential centers, vocational programs, or other programs designed to meet the needs of individuals with developmental disabilities. Caregivers act not only as providers for children but as advocates, liaisons, and collaborators on behalf of the child to the outside world. This is especially true for children, adolescents, and young adults with developmental disabilities.

Self-Care

Appropriate self-care is essential for caregivers and is often overlooked, especially as it may be challenging to focus on self-care if caregivers do not have others to help them or others who can supervise their child. Caring for a child, adolescent, or young adult with developmental disabilities is especially taxing on a caregiver who likely spends an exorbitant amount of time, energy, and money on caring for a child with a variety of emotional, social, behavioral, and medical needs. Furthermore, self-care for caregivers following disclosure of sexual abuse of their child is paramount as this can create a large amount of distress. Additionally, caregivers are easily taken for granted by others, thus it may often feel like a thankless role. Caregivers may be used to putting themselves last and often ignore their own needs; however, this can lead to burnout, distress, and overall stress, mood, and anxiety problems. It is important to acknowledge and encourage caregivers to engage in activities that help restore their energy, emotional, and spiritual needs. Clinicians may choose to address this topic alone with a caregiver to help them fully understand and appreciate the importance of self-care. Examples of self-care activities may include taking a hot shower, gardening, spending time with friends, or getting a massage. Additionally, caregivers within the foster care system can request respite services while other caregivers can seek out babysitters or alternate caregivers to allow themselves time for self-care. All caregivers should be informed of any special supervision needs of the child or adolescent, including if there is an active supervision plan in place due to a child's disruptive or inappropriate behaviors with others. It is important to remember caregivers are better able to care for others when they care for themselves.

Participation in Treatment

Caregivers must be active participants in trauma-focused therapy to understand how abuse impacts the survivor. Essential knowledge and skills are provided to caregivers on ways they can aid their child in healing but also to help and support caregivers in processing their thoughts, feelings, and reactions to their child's abuse. Caregivers can support their child at home and practice skills learned in therapy. Examples include behavior management skills to help reduce maladaptive behaviors and increase adaptive behaviors exhibited by their child. While the therapist reviews and practices these skills during therapy sessions, caregivers must practice and reinforce skills learned in treatment at home to help the child generalize these behaviors to daily life. If a caregiver is resistant or ambivalent to participating in trauma-focused treatment the child will likely struggle in therapy or make minimal or short-lived gains.

The Role of Schools: Resources, Accommodations

Caregivers must act as advocates and liaisons within the school setting. Children and adolescents with developmental disabilities qualify to receive special education services and accommodations within the school setting, depending on their needs. Most often a special education plan is called an Individualized Education Plan (IEP) in which the child or adolescent's level of functioning is evaluated and appropriate accommodations are provided based on the evaluation, such as occupational therapy services, social work services, or academic accommodations. Additionally, supervision and/or safety plans are included in IEPs to ensure the safety of the child at school as well as the safety of peers. There are a variety of less structured and less formal accommodations a child may receive at school; thus, it is part of the caregiver's role to learn what educational rights their child has as well as follow-up with school personnel to determine if appropriate accommodations are being received. Some schools and school districts may be ill-equipped to serve the needs of a child with a developmental disability, depending on the child's level of functioning and specialized needs. Specialty schools, such as therapeutic schools, may be a viable option to ensure appropriate services are received by the child or adolescent. Special education services and accommodations are available for young adults who attend college courses as well. Furthermore, caregivers need to act as advocates for accommodations related to medical disabilities or difficulties within the school or vocational setting.

Caregivers must collaborate and act as liaisons with teachers and other school personnel. Caregivers can sign a two-way release of information authorizing therapists to communicate with the child or adolescent's teachers and school staff to ensure that appropriate accommodations are provided for the student. The therapist can share psychoeducation on trauma, the child's condition, collaborate with the school's social worker or counselor, and aid teachers in the use of techniques for emotional management as needed. Caregivers should regularly communicate with school personnel who come into the most contact with their child to receive daily reports on their child's functioning as well as provide the personnel with relevant information on the child's mood and behaviors that day, i.e., if the child slept poorly he or she may be irritable the next day at school. Additionally, caregivers can report back any noticeable changes in behavior or mood at school or home to the therapist as trauma-informed treatment may increase disruptive behaviors in some children. Keeping open communication allows the therapist to make appropriate modifications if disruptive behaviors or a decrease in mood is noted by caregivers or teachers.

Family Support

While caregiver self-care was mentioned previously, it is important to focus on the care and support of the family members within the child's system. This may include but it is not limited to siblings, grandparents, aunts or uncles, cousins, and close friends. Family members of children, adolescents, and young adults who experienced trauma experience their own reaction to the abuse of their family member as well as to a shift in family dynamics. Family members of survivors with developmental disabilities may require additional support related to the individual's specific condition, i.e., medical, cognitive, or physical.

Family therapy can be one option for families in order to address and support an entire system of individuals within the child's life. Additionally, group therapy or support groups are available for siblings, parents, grandparents, or other family members and support people.

Chapter 7

ADJUNCT TREATMENTS AND SERVICES

Evaluation/Testing

Effective trauma-based therapy for children, adolescents, and young adults with developmental disabilities includes a review of previous testing or psychological/neuropsychological testing reports, if available, prior to or during the beginning stages of treatment, as discussed in this workbook previously. A trauma-based assessment or brief evaluation serves to initiate trauma-focused clinical services to identify the impact of sexual abuse on the individual's level of functioning as well as clarify mental health diagnoses and treatment needs, including accommodations made in treatment to facilitate the individual's trauma treatment most effectively. It is recommended that clinicians continue to evaluate the individual's level of progress as well as symptoms throughout treatment with the use of appropriate outcome measures, such as a trauma symptom measure. However, there are times when treatment has begun but due to a decrease in functioning, change in medical/physical status, environmental change, or change in symptom presentation, a child may need to be referred for a more extensive or comprehensive assessment or psychological/neuropsychological testing to best inform subsequent treatment. Depending on the child's presentation and circumstances of treatment, therapy may continue during further evaluation or pause, if appropriate, until the findings of the evaluation/assessment are reviewed and treatment accommodations and/or appropriate referrals are made.

Group Therapy

There are a variety of groups that individuals who experienced trauma can benefit from attending while attending individual and family therapy services. Examples of appropriate groups can include social skill groups, especially for children with developmental disabilities who have significant social skill difficulties. Individuals with developmental disabilities have access to a variety of other group therapy experiences if placed in a therapeutic school, residential facility, or require specialized services through their IEP. These groups can include, but are not limited to, emotional regulation groups, art therapy, music therapy, and occupational therapy.

Caregivers and family members also benefit from group therapy while engaged in trauma-focused therapy for their child. Examples include caregiver or sibling support groups aimed at education and skill-building, as well as support. Additionally, psychoeducational or support groups related to a child's specific diagnosis or disability are beneficial for family members to increase knowledge and understanding of a child's unique strengths and difficulties.

Psychiatric Services and Level of Care (LOC)

For moderate to severe trauma conditions, certain trauma specific psychiatric medications are helpful and necessary. Clinicians can recommend a psychiatric medication evaluation and/or consult with a psychiatrist with experience working with individuals in the developmentally disabled population when necessary. Additionally, clinicians educate and empower caregivers about creating a collaborative relationship with psychiatrists. Be aware that people can neurochemically improve their affect dysregulation from antidepressants and mood stabilizers, but not from benzodiazepines and sedatives. Managing sleep with medications can improve overall functioning. Additionally, if symptoms become severe or increase in intensity or frequency, it is important to consider the appropriate level of care for each individual. Some individuals require higher levels of care at times, including shorter-term intensive outpatient, partial hospitalization, or inpatient hospitalization programs. Furthermore, longer-term residential and therapeutic schools are additional treatment options. No matter what adjunct treatments or services are provided, clinicians need to collaborate with outside providers to coordinate care. As stated earlier in this workbook, clinicians must obtain a signed release of information to communicate with an outside professional.

Occupational/Physical Therapy

Due to potential sensory processing and/or integration difficulties as well as physical concerns related to some conditions such as autism spectrum disorders or Cerebral Palsy, adjunct treatment may include occupational and/or physical therapy. While these two treatments are often lumped together, occupational and physical therapies can serve different purposes. Occupational therapy is generally focused on specific goals to increase the individual's ability to perform tasks related to daily living or to increase daily functioning. Occupational therapy can also be utilized for sensory concerns. Physical therapy is generally focused on repairing or improving physical impairments.

Speech Therapy

Speech therapy is utilized for individuals with communication disorders or difficulties. It is conducted by speech and language pathologists with specialized knowledge and training in this area. Many children, adolescents, and young adults with developmental disabilities require speech therapy services, i.e., lower functioning child on the autism spectrum, may receive services with a specialized provider with an outside agency or school in conjunction with trauma-focused counseling services. Speech therapy accommodations can also be required by law in IEPs at school. Please note that this adjunct treatment is meant for individuals who struggle with communication prior to trauma. Some survivors may experience a decrease in communication following abuse or a traumatic experience but this does not necessarily constitute the need for speech therapy services as the communication deficit is likely related to a reaction to trauma rather than a true communication disorder. A specialized speech evaluation may be required to determine service needs.

School Counselors and Social Workers

Many children and adolescents with developmental disabilities and emotional or behavioral difficulties are likely to receive counseling services from a school counselor or social worker. This adjunct provider can be a great collaborative resource for clinicians in engaging the child in trauma-focused therapy and bridging treatment interventions to school. The child may see the school counselor or social worker as part of his or her IEP, or simply as needed. These professionals provide a wealth of knowledge regarding the child's school and social functioning and can serve as active collaborators with teachers and other educational professionals within the school setting. They act as secondary sources of information related to the family's functioning level and engagement with educational services. Outside the school, counseling services are important as school counselors and social workers generally do not address abuse or other non-academic/school topics or areas.

Medical

Depending on the individual's conditions, he or she may receive multiple services from a variety of medical professionals. These medical professionals may include developmental pediatricians, physician specialists, or neurologists. It is important for clinicians to gain a thorough medical history of each individual, as well as obtain contact information and signed releases of information with medical professionals to collaborate the individual's care. Clinicians must be aware of possible medical trauma depending on the child's experience with medical treatment and procedures, especially painful or invasive procedures, as this would be an important component to include in trauma-focused treatment.

Individuals with developmental disabilities may have a higher rate of food allergies and sensitivities than individuals in the general population. If these issues are not addressed, they can impact a child's behavioral and social-emotional functioning. Some children require adjunct treatment with registered dieticians to develop an appropriate nutritional plan. Furthermore, if sensory issues are present some children with developmental disabilities may be extremely picky eaters or struggle to gain adequate calories or nutrition, thus requiring outside treatment with a registered dietician, speech and language pathologist specializing in feeding, feeding therapist, and any other applicable medical professionals. Clinicians should note that appetite changes can increase or result from exposure to sexual abuse or trauma for any child and thus should be appropriately assessed.

Animal-Assisted Therapy

There are numerous therapists, counselors, and schools which utilize animal-assisted therapy, also known as pet therapy. This approach entails a trained professional who handles a trained animal, generally a dog, to engage therapeutically with children with developmental disabilities and/or children with social-emotional difficulties. Animal-assisted therapy is found in hospitals, where appropriate. While animal-assisted therapy is generally not a long-term adjunct treatment, some individuals with developmental disabilities are exposed to this type of therapy. Animal-assisted therapy is beneficial in that there are no social or communication demands placed on the child in order to interact with the therapeutic pet.

Therapeutic Massage/Yoga

Therapeutic massage and yoga, as well as additional body-focused treatments, are helpful adjunct treatments to trauma-focused treatment. Besides an increased connection and integration of body and mind, both modalities aim to alleviate or reduce distressful physical symptoms, such as muscular rigidity associated with Cerebral Palsy. Professionals should take note of possible sensory issues that impact therapeutic massage and yoga, as well as consider the possibility of retriggering traumatic memories in yoga or with massage touching.

Chapter 8

PREVENTION STRATEGIES

Prevention strategies and programs are helpful to reduce the risk of victimization in children and adolescents. While there are numerous programs aimed at adults with developmental disabilities, there are few if any accessible prevention programs for children and adolescents with developmental disabilities to reduce the risk of sexual abuse and victimization. Caregivers are often left without prevention strategies or support as well. This population suffers from a lack of education regarding healthy sexuality as individuals with developmental disabilities are often stigmatized as "asexual." It is helpful to address prevention strategies with a two-prong approach, the first prong being teaching children, adolescents, and young adults prevention skills and the second prong being teaching caregivers these skills.

Some of the most important components of any prevention strategy aimed at reducing the risk of sexual abuse or victimization of children, adolescents, and young adults with developmental disabilities is awareness, education, and safety skills. It is of utmost importance that these individuals learn about their bodies, anatomy, and sexuality in healthy and pro-social ways. Caregivers act as a primary source of education to these children. There are a number of books or similar resources available to provide age-appropriate and developmentally-appropriate language for caregivers to use. Children and adolescents should be taught the appropriate anatomical names of body parts and demonstrate the ability to identify private parts or sexual parts of their body (although uncomfortable touch can occur anywhere on the body). This knowledge allows children a basic understanding that their body belongs to them, as well as provides the language for children to report any instances of inappropriate sexual touching or uncomfortable touch they may experience. Prevention programs should also include education regarding healthy sexuality, development, and puberty as well as definitions of sexual abuse. When a child or adolescent is aware of what sexual abuse is, they can identify the behavior as wrong, inappropriate, and illegal which increases the chance the child will use the safety skills described below, as well as report any incident to an appropriate authority, i.e., caretaker.

Secondly, safety skills must be a focus of any prevention program. Safety skills include giving the child, adolescent, and young adult permission to say no to any uncomfortable touch, from any adult, caretaker, or peer. Prevention programs can utilize role-play or social stories to aid the child in practicing saying no to another person. Of course, role-plays would not include actual inappropriate touch but can simply aid the child in saying the word "no" with appropriate tone, volume, and nonverbal behaviors, such as eye contact, that send an even more powerful message to a potential offender and will likely reduce the risk of victimization. The individual should learn how to get away from the potentially dangerous person and/or situation and to tell an appropriate authority. Each child or adolescent should create a list of appropriate adults to tell as well as be reminded to keep telling adults until someone believes them. Caretakers should participate in prevention programs to improve their knowledge and skill set to better protect their children but also to learn how to respond appropriately to any disclosure or potentially risky situation.

Finally, caregivers need to actively check-in with their children on a regular basis to increase communication and the child's comfort level in speaking with a trusted adult. This acts as a good reminder to children that their caregiver is attuned and actively participating in the child's safety, as well as reminds the child of the education and skills learned related to prevention.

Part II

THERAPEUTIC WORKSHEETS, ACTIVITIES, AND INTERVENTIONS FOR TT-CAYDD

INTRODUCTION TO THE WORKSHEETS

The following worksheets are designed and intended to help clinicians address aspects of trauma treatment with children, adolescents, and young adults with developmental disabilities. They can serve as examples and tools to help guide and facilitate trauma treatment with this population. The worksheets have been written at various reading levels to meet the needs of a wide range of clients, and therefore, clinicians should modify and utilize them and use them in their trauma treatment at client-appropriate levels. A variety of reading levels were used intentionally to use this workbook with a larger group of clients of varying ages and developmental levels. These modules are flexible in that they do not need to be used in the exact order presented as the clinician must assess what order best meets their client's needs, however, the order presented is the suggested sequence of treatment components.

PSYCHOEDUCATION WORKSHEETS

PSYCHOEDUCATION WORKSHEETS

Welcome to therapy! Therapy is a place where you can share your thoughts and feelings with your therapist. Your therapist is here to help you feel better and learn skills so you can help yourself feel better! Sometimes therapy may seem scary or make you nervous, but your therapist is here to help you learn about yourself, your feelings, and both good and bad things that have happened to you.

For Clinicians: Utilize a feelings chart to aide in identifying feelings. Individuals can point to feelings rather than drawing or writing, especially if there are motor issues present as in Cerebral Palsy. In the case of communication challenges, facilitate this information in another format and paraphrase information as needed.

What questions do you have about therapy? Draw or write them below:

Your therapist will help you learn a lot about yourself and will teach you about a lot of new things! Can you think of some good things about yourself to share with your therapist? You can write them out or draw a picture in the clouds below. You can use the next page, too!

Why do you think you are you coming to therapy? Draw or write below:

Many people come to therapy for many different reasons. There are many kids, teens, and adults who experience something bad that happened to them and it makes them feel bad. Feeling bad can mean having nightmares or scary dreams, feeling unsafe, nervous, or scared or feeling mad and angry. Your therapist has worked with many people to help them feel better. In what ways have you felt bad?

What are some things that make you feel good? Draw or write them below!

What will you do in therapy? Read the options below and circle which ones you think you may do in therapy.

Talk about your feelings

Learn ways to feel better

Play games

Be safe

Work with your therapist to think of some more things you may do in therapy and draw or write them below. You can use the next page, too!

Have you ever heard of the word "trauma?" Trauma is something that happens to you, or that you may see, that can make you feel very scared, nervous, or bad. It might feel scary to think about or remember a trauma that happened. Many children experience one or more traumas, **YOU ARE NOT ALONE!** Draw a picture of how you feel learning about trauma:

There are many different types of trauma. For example, natural disasters (like tornados or earthquakes) can be very scary and traumatic. (Ask your therapist what "*traumatic means.*")

Work with your therapist to think of other types of trauma.

Sexual abuse is one type of trauma. Sexual abuse is when an adult (or an older child or teen) touches a younger child's private parts (body parts covered by your bathing suit) or has a child touch their private parts. Or, even if the child or teens are the same age, if one person does not understand what is going on.

This can be very scary and it is **NEVER** the child's fault.

Sexual abuse can cause a lot of confusing thoughts and feelings. Read some of the sentences below and *choose if the sentence if true or false about sexual abuse*, your therapist can help you!

1. Sexual abuse is the kid's fault	Yes	No
2. Many people experience sexual abuse	Yes	No
3. Family members or friends can sexually abuse a child	Yes	No
4. If I was sexually abused it means I am a bad person	Yes	No

You are doing a great job with your workbook! Learning about trauma and sexual abuse can be hard but that is why you have your therapist to help you! *What are some ways your therapist can help you?* Draw or write them below:

What are some fun things that you like to do?

Alright, you are doing a great job in your workbook! What have you learned so far? Draw or write below:

AFFECT REGULATION WORKSHEETS

AFFECT REGULATION WORKSHEETS

There are many different feelings a person can have. Look at the list of feeling words below and circle the feelings that you are having now.

For Clinicians: A feelings chart with faces depicting different feelings may be helpful for less verbal clients and can be found on the next page. Also, the use of a mirror or therapeutic games focused on feelings may be helpful in understanding, exploring, and identifying feelings.

confident	happy	playful	calm	courageous	energetic	free
optimistic	lucky	comfortable	encouraged	impulsive	blessed	glad
interested	surprised	satisfied	thankful	important	sympathetic	quiet
challenged	bright	reassured	loving	eager	affected	sure
affectionate	sensitive	devoted	passionate	warm	loved	nosy
curious	anxious	inspired	determined	excited	heartbroken	kind
hopeful	certain	rebellious	powerless	secure	irritated	guilty
enraged	hostile	annoyed	hateful	dissatisfied	unique	upset
disappointed	discouraged	ashamed	miserable	indecisive	uncertain	bad
shy	hesitant	embarrassed	incapable	alone	fatigued	useless
inferior	vulnerable	empty	doubtful	aggressive	resentful	angry
provoked	disgusting	terrible	unpleasant	skeptical	distrustful	unsure
dominated	pessimistic	uneasy	tense	frustrated	distressed	dull
pathetic	neutral	weary	bored	distracted	cold	lost
disinterested	terrified	suspicious	anxious	alarmed	panic	scared
nervous	worried	frightened	rejected	injured	offended	tearful
doubtful	desperate	unhappy	lonely	shaky	restless	grief
threatened	victimized	appalled	humiliated	wronged	alienated	brave

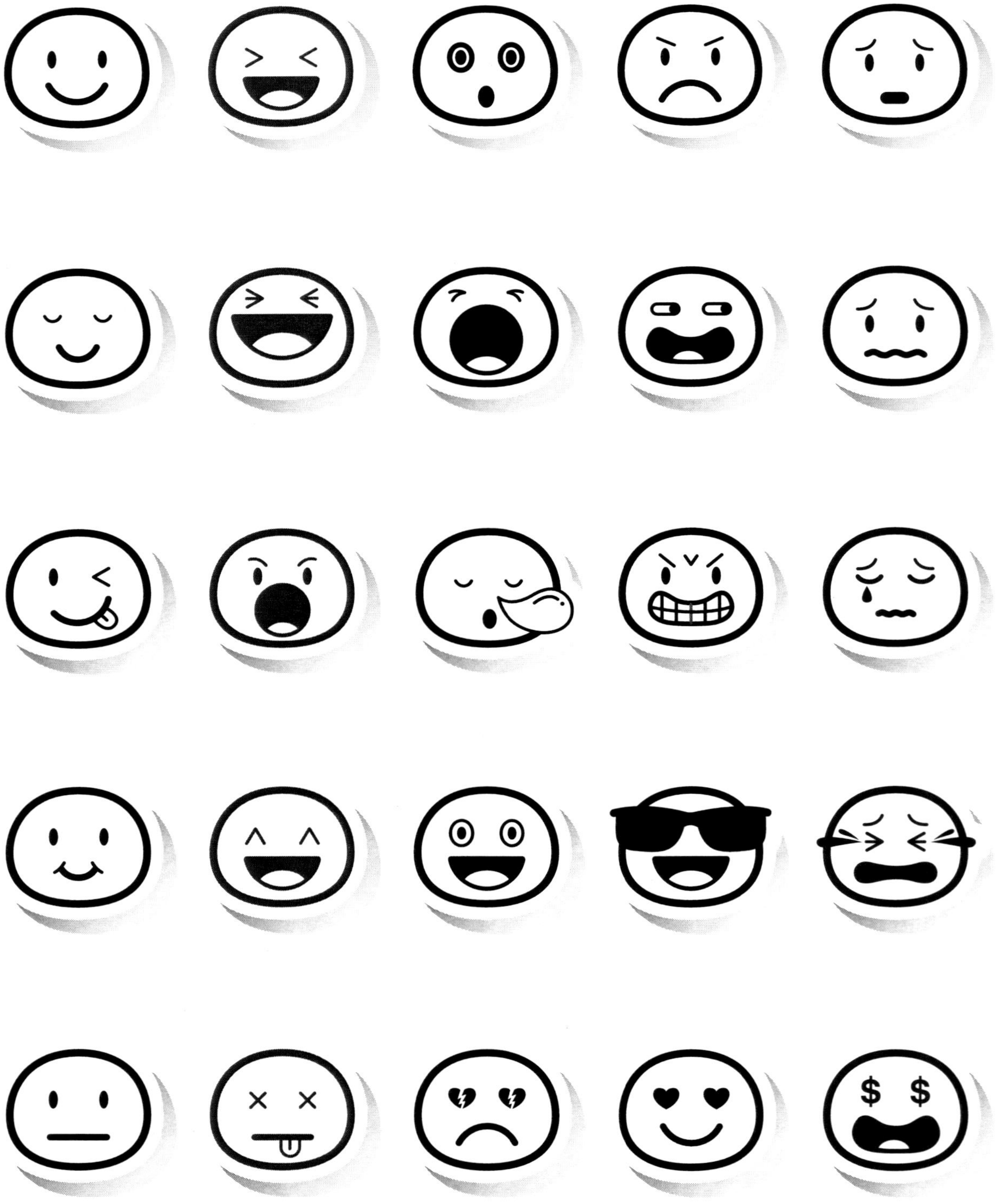

Here is an outline different body types. Take a few moments to scan your body for any tension. Circle the areas where you feel tension the most. Using a different colored pen, circle where you feel body sensations when you are experiencing strong feelings. Refer to the next sheet for ideas if needed. Notice if the areas you have circled in different colors are the same or different. Discuss this with your therapist.

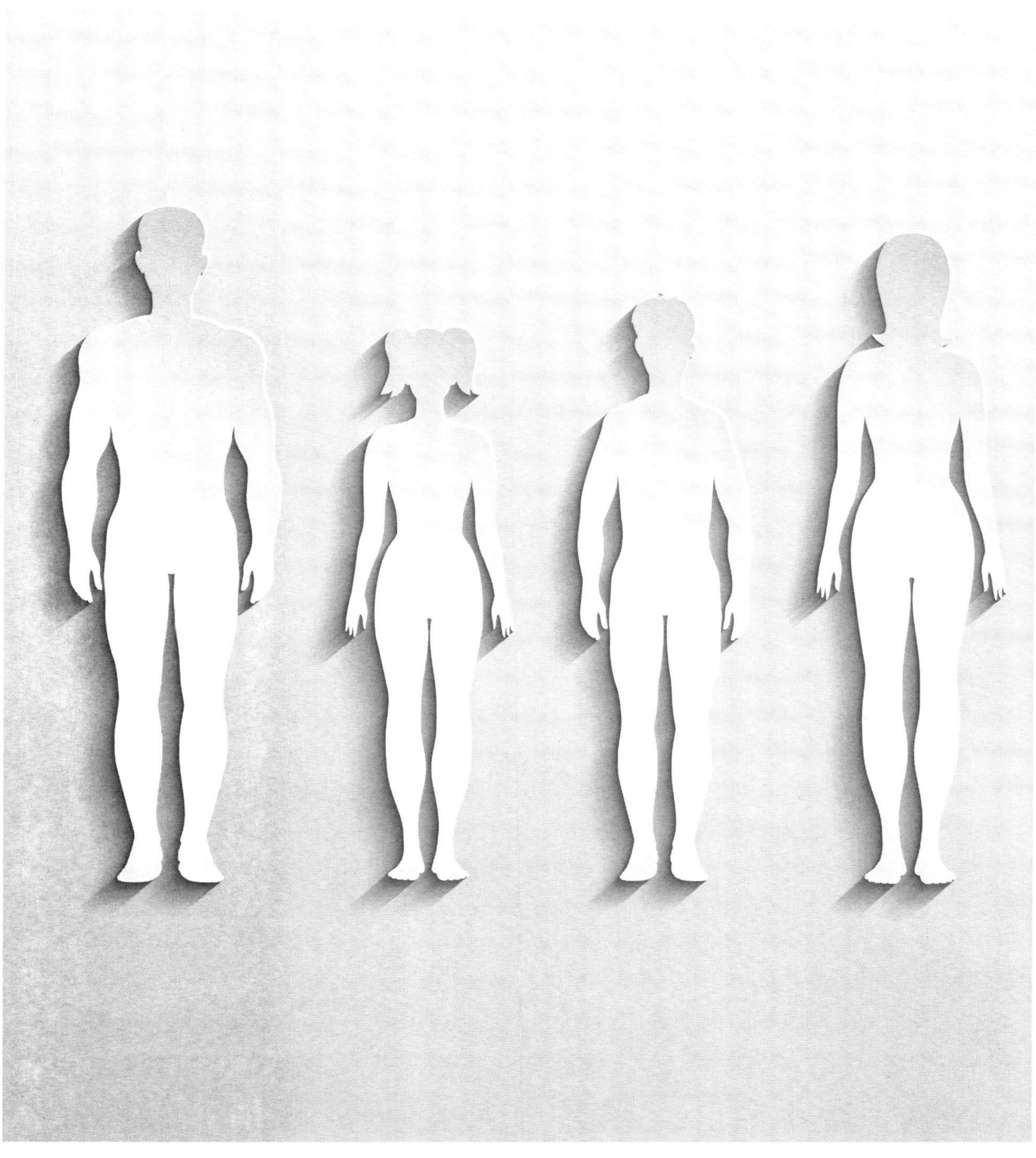

BODILY OR PHYSICAL SIGNS OF STRESS

- Muscle tension
- Neck pain
- Cold/sweaty hands
- Facial movements
- Tired
- Headaches
- Indigestion or stomach pain
- Fast heart beat
- Back pain

BEHAVIORAL SIGNS OF STRESS

- Can't eat or eat too much
- Forget things
- Yelling
- Physical aggression
- Can't work
- Don't want to be around people or talk to them
- Drink more caffeine or smoke tobacco more
- Can't make decisions
- Can't pay attention

ACCEPTING YOUR FEELINGS

You are going to have all kinds of feelings. This is part of being a person. When you accept your feelings, you are recognizing yourself as a person.

Accepting your feelings means being willing and able to accept and feel your feelings, especially the negative ones. When you do this, you are agreeing or admitting that your feelings are happening and letting yourself feel them. Doing this helps you in many ways. By admitting to your feelings, you are accepting yourself and the situation. You don't have to spend more time or energy pushing your feelings away. Instead, once your feelings are accepted by you, you can use your coping skills, release your feelings, and continue with your day to day and life goals.

Other ways that accepting or admitting to your feelings helps is that you are taking an opportunity or chance to learn about your feelings and learn new ways to manage them that are better for you, and you become a new and better person. When you push your feelings away, you don't learn these things or grow and change, because you can't learn or become something by not doing it.

Finally, when you learn to accept your feelings, you begin to say to yourself, "Things are not that bad," "I can manage this," and "Things will get better for me." When you have bad feelings, they are not nice to experience, but they cannot destroy your life. When they become more annoying and less overwhelming, you are less afraid to experience them and they become much easier for you to handle. When you push your feelings away instead, your feelings can become extremely overwhelming to your body, and they can come out in other ways and cause many problems for you. Accepting your feelings allows your feelings to be expressed and helps you move freely through your days and life, while pushing feelings away blocks the flow of your feelings and your experiences in life.

For Clinicians: Read and process this page with your client. Help your client think of examples. Make sure to modify as appropriate for your client.

COPING SKILLS

The following suggested coping skills are separated into two categories: relaxation tools and active tools to calm down. It is likely that you tend to respond to one of these two approaches better than the other. You may need to try a few coping skill activities from each category to understand which type is more effective for you. You may think of many other tools that are not listed here as well. Review the following tools and others you may think of with your therapist. Your therapist can help you practice and learn more about each tool.

Relaxation Tools

Breathing Tools such as deep breathing

Muscle Relaxation which may include tensing and releasing various muscles groups in a systematic way

Mindfulness where you focus attention on the present moment, without judgment

Visualization and Guided Imagery exercises

Active Tools to Calm Down

1. Journal or write about your thoughts and feelings
2. Talk to someone
3. Play or do something you enjoy
4. Reorganize or redecorate your living space
5. Do a physical exercise like jumping jacks or running in place
6. Sing a song
7. Do a spiritual activity
8. Do something you'd really like to do for yourself
9. Change into comfortable clothes
10. Dance
11. Take a bath or shower
12. Play with a pet
13. Count forward or backward
14. Listen to music
15. Draw a picture or create something using your hands

YOUR TOOLS

COGNITIVE WORKSHEETS

COGNITIVE WORKSHEETS

Now it is time to learn more about thoughts! Thoughts are words, sentences, or pictures we get in our heads that only we can hear. Can you think of any examples? List them below; your therapist can help you!

Everyone has thoughts, both good and not so good thoughts. Good thoughts are thoughts that make us feel happy or give us positive feelings when we think of them. List some examples below:

Not so good thoughts are thoughts that we have that give us negative feelings. We also have not so good thoughts sometimes. What are some of your not so good thoughts? Draw or write below:

Did you know that people who experience trauma, especially sexual abuse, can have a lot of not so good thoughts that pop into their head? Although it might feel scary *it is normal to have bad thoughts when something bad happened to you.* What bad thoughts about your trauma do you have?

Good job sharing! Even though it may feel like bad thoughts will never go away your therapist is here to help you learn how to fight your bad thoughts. You can do it! Work with your therapist to make a list of what tools you have and tools you can learn to help fight your bad thoughts.

Tools I have:

Tools I will learn:

Excellent! One tool that you can use is distraction. Distraction is when you think of something that makes you feel good when a bad thought pops into your head. What can you think of to help fight a bad thought? Draw or write below.

One great distraction is thinking of a **safe or happy place**. Your therapist will help you with this.

For Clinicians: Help your client utilize imagery as a distraction technique. First, instruct the client to think of a place where he/she feels safe, it could be somewhere real or imaginary. Next, instruct the client to close his/her eyes or keep them open if preferred and imagine this safe place in his/her mind. Help the client notice and review all the details of the safe place, such as what he/she can see, hear, smell, taste, and feel. Don't forget to have the client give the safe place a name! Or represent the image with art.

Circle what feelings you had when you thought about your safe place? Write the feeling word below the feeling face! Your therapist can help you with feeling words.

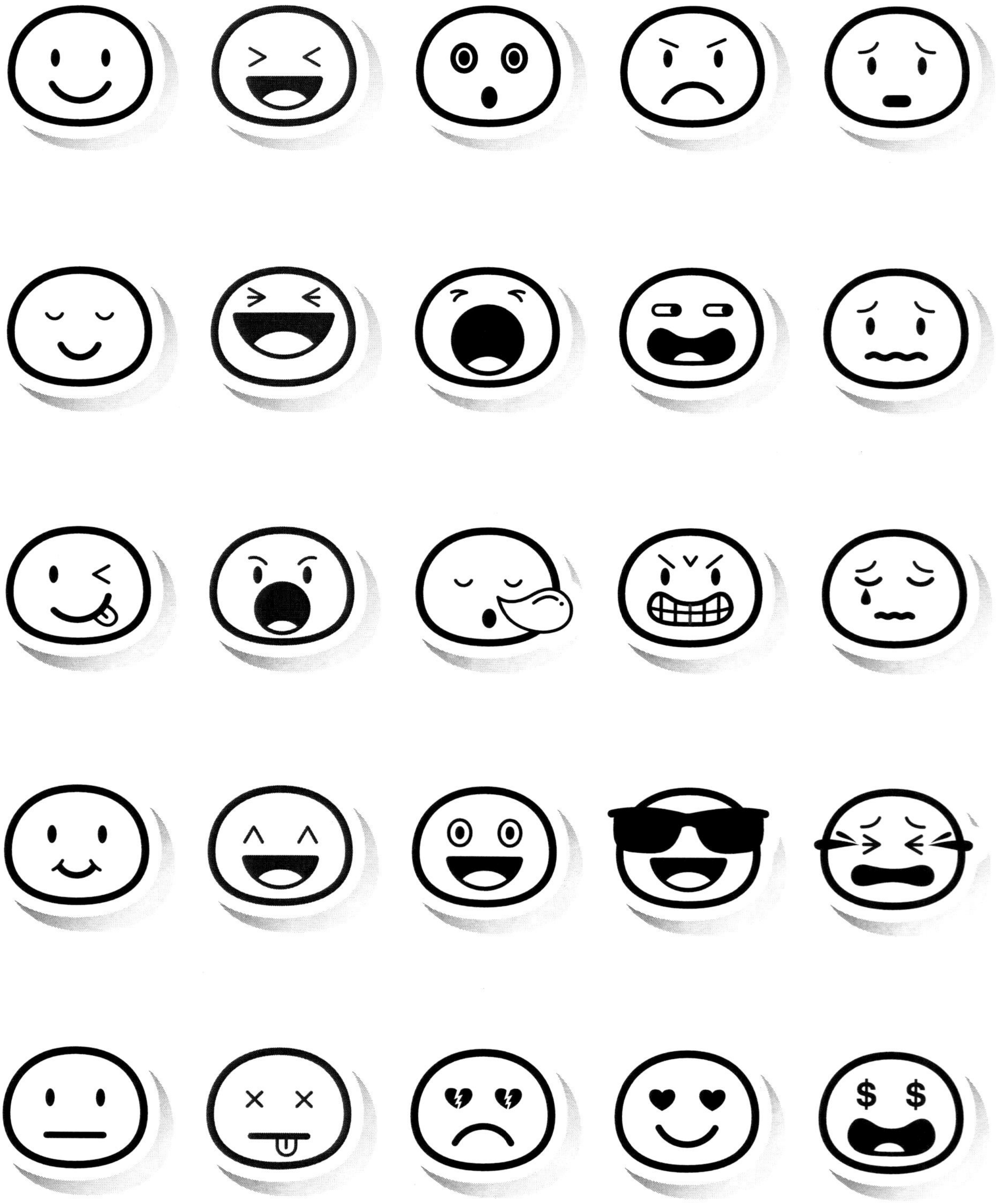

Great! Now, you can use either this paper (and the next page too!) or your therapist can get a bigger piece of paper where you can draw your safe place. Don't forget to give your safe place a name!

Your picture came out great! Now, your therapist can help you practice thinking of your safe place to fight bad thoughts. Your safe place can also help fight bad feelings! After your therapist helps you practice thinking of your safe place, circle the faces which show how you are feeling now:

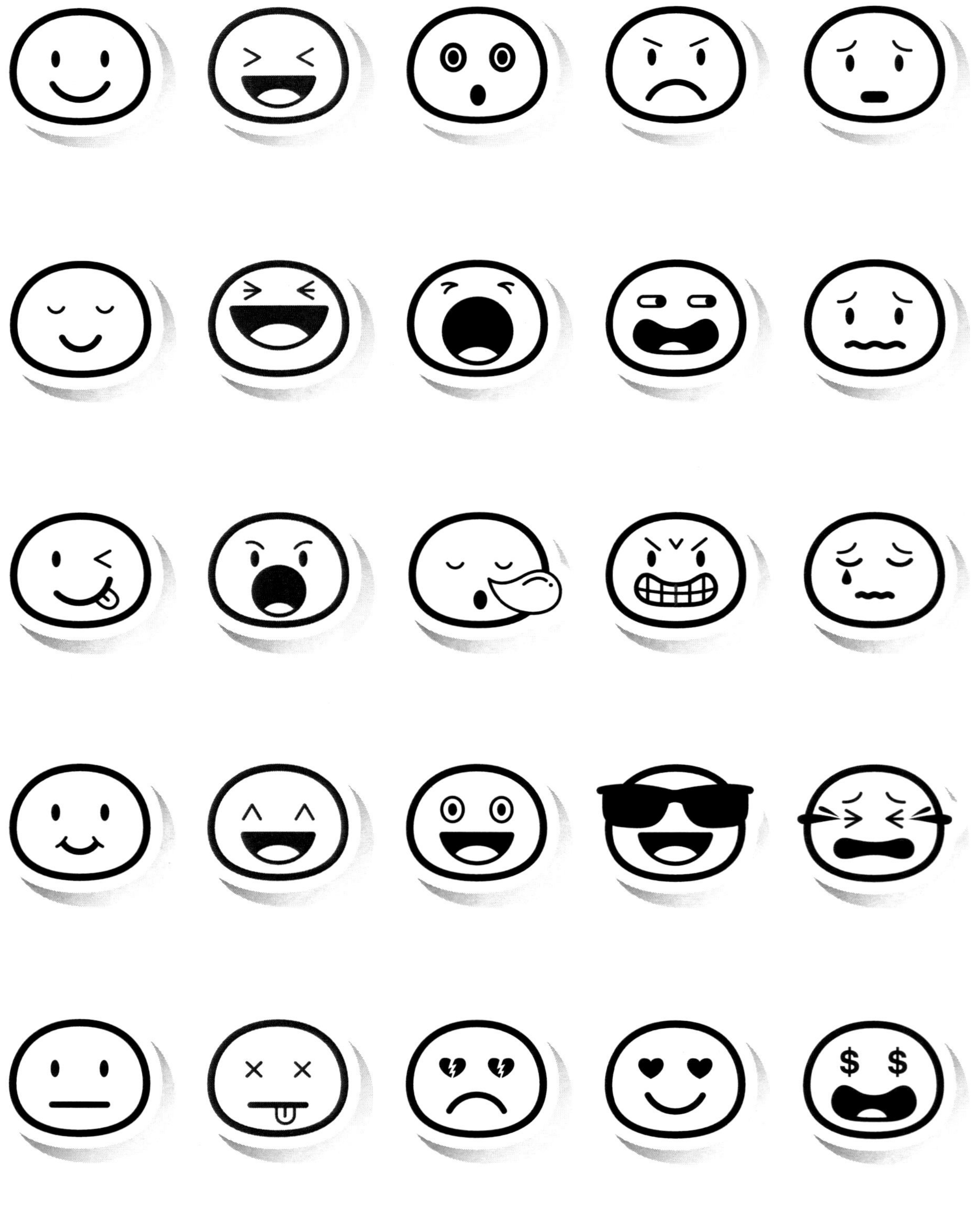

You have done great job learning about trauma, feelings, thoughts, and ways to help yourself feel better if an emotion gets too strong! Now your therapist is going to help you learn more about yourself! Draw or write down some things you like about yourself below:

What about things you may not like about yourself? It is normal to not like everything about yourself but sometimes when someone experiences a trauma it can make them not like a lot of different things and make them feel bad or confused about themselves.

Now draw or write things that make you different from other people.

Use the space below to draw or write about things that you are good at or enjoy doing:

Do you remember when we learned that sometimes when a kid, teen, or adult experiences sexual abuse it can give them confusing thoughts? One confusing thought a lot of people have is about their bodies and who is in charge (control) of their bodies. Some people get confused about who is the boss of their bodies. Who is in control, or the boss, of your body? Draw who is the boss of your body here:

Although it may feel confusing at times, ***YOU** are the boss of your body.* Your body belongs to you. This can be confusing if someone else has hurt your body. Your therapist will help you learn different ways to help keep your body safe and will talk to you more about **YOU** being the boss of your body! Now, draw who is the boss of your body here:

You are learning so much! What questions do you have so far?

COPING SKILLS WORKSHEETS

COPING SKILLS WORKSHEETS

The following pages are designed for you to list your coping skills with the help of your therapist. These are skills you can use at home, at school, and when you are out in the community. Once you have completed your list of coping skills, your list can be copied and copies of your list can be posted in many areas of your home, such as your bedroom, the bathroom, and the kitchen and living room, and at school in your school locker and school folder, and in your pocket for when you are out in the community. Having your list with you or around you can help remind you to use your coping skills. Be sure to share this list with the people you live with so that they can support and help you to remember to use them when you might need them. If you try one coping skill on your list and it doesn't work, try using a different one from your list. Keep doing this until one of the coping skills on your list works. Be sure to pat yourself on the back when you use your coping skills! The people that you live with can also provide you with positive rewards for doing this!

"MY COPING SHEET"

1. ______________________________

____

____

2. ______________________________

____

____

3. ______________________________

____

____

4. ______________________________

____

____

5. ______________________________

____

____

6. ______________________________

____

____

7. ______________________________

____

____

COPING SKILLS JOURNAL SHEET

Below is a chart for keeping track or journaling when you needed coping skills and what coping skills you used. When you fill out this chart each day and read it when it is completed, it will help you know which coping skills worked best and which ones to use in the future. You can earn rewards for using your coping skills.

When? (Time of day, During a specific activity, etc.)	**Where? (Place)**	**What Coping Skill Was Used? (Refer to your coping skill list)**	**Was it Helpful? (Rate it, 1-5):** **1=not helpful, 3=sort of helpful 5=very helpful**	**Why do you think it was helpful or not helpful?**

SELF-AWARENESS AND MINDFULNESS WORKSHEETS

SELF-AWARENESS AND MINDFULNESS WORKSHEETS

Now that you learned about some of the confusing thoughts people may have about their bodies or themselves after sexual abuse, we are going to learn about some of the confusing feelings kids may have inside their bodies. After a trauma, many kids may feel sick later, like having headaches, stomachaches, or feeling tired. What body feelings did you have?

A lot of times the feelings you may have inside your body may feel scary or remind you of the bad or scary thing that happened. That is normal for people who experienced a trauma, but it is important to remember that your body belongs to ______________________ (fill in the blank).

Although it might feel scary at first, it is important to pay attention to your body, feelings, and thoughts. Your therapist has already helped you learn different tools to help you when your feelings get too strong. Another tool to learn is called mindfulness.

Mindfulness means that you pay attention to the way that you are feeling or thoughts that you have or what is happening inside your body without thinking of them as bad or good. You just notice them. This is something that takes practice but you can do it! Your therapist will help you learn how to pay attention or be mindful right now!

<u>For Clinicians</u>: Use the sample script on the next page to introduce mindfulness to your client. Please adjust accordingly to consider any physical disabilities or medical conditions.

Sample Mindfulness Script

Make sure to sit or position your body in a comfortable position. You can close your eyes if you feel comfortable, and if not, that is okay. If you choose to keep your eyes open please focus on one object or space in the room.

We are going to begin by taking deep breaths. Breathe in through your nose, hold your breath to my count, and breathe out through your mouth. Let's practice. Breathe in 2-3-4, hold 2-3-4, breathe out 2-3-4. Great. (Repeat for 5 deep breaths.) Now we are going to practice breathing this way but I want you practice counting the numbers yourself in your head as you breath. (Repeat for 5 deep breaths.) Excellent!

You are doing such a great job. Now that we have learned a great way to take deep breaths lets focus our attention on the breath. This time as you breathe in, notice how the air moves up your nostrils. Breathe in . . . hold . . . breathe out. As the air passes down your nostrils notice how it moves down to your lungs, inflating your lungs with air. Let's take a moment to notice how the air moves from the nostrils to the lungs. (Pause for a moment of breathing.)

Now let's focus on the out-breath. This time bring your attention to the air flow as you breathe out, noticing how the air moves out of your mouth and over your lips as your lungs deflate. Continue to focus on the out-breath for the next moment.

Great, your body should continue to feel relaxed as you bring your attention to your breath. Thoughts may enter your mind, let them pass as you focus on your breath. Let's take five deep breaths with your attention to each stage of the breath. (Pause for five deep breaths.) When you are ready slowly bring your attention back to the current space, open your eyes slowly, and notify me when you are done with this exercise.

How did that feel? Draw or write below:

For Clinicians: Help the child process their thoughts, feelings, and reactions associated with the mindfulness exercise. Be aware that children who experienced sexual abuse may have a variety of physical reactions or physical triggers when focusing inward on their internal experiences, make sure to acknowledge, normalize, and process.

TRAUMA STORY WORKSHEETS

TRAUMA STORY WORKSHEETS

Trauma Reprocessing and the Trauma Story: A Worksheet for Clinicians to Guide this Process

A trauma story or narrative is widely used in trauma-focused treatment and can act as an exposure technique as well as provide opportunities for an individual to further integrate and process their trauma. A trauma story can take many forms such as written, verbal, or art, however, no matter the form the purpose is for the child to "tell their story." The level of detail in a trauma story may vary although there are several important components to consider such as including thoughts, feelings, and events relevant to the abuse as well as creating a beginning, middle, and end to the narrative. A child may choose to start their story at any point in time they wish and can include hopes and plans for the future as the end of their story. Children with chronic or complex abuse histories can choose a specific incidence of abuse in which they want to feel better.

The trauma story is presented when a child has sufficient knowledge regarding trauma and demonstrates effective copping skills, as this module in treatment has the potential to increase disruptive behaviors or trigger anxiety symptoms. Caregivers are an important part of this module as the goal is for them to eventually witness and support their child's story. Some children may need these sessions to be highly structured and include a transition in and out of session. The therapist should help the child process thoughts and feelings associated with writing and expressing their trauma story.

RECOMMENDED GUIDELINES FOR CLINICIANS:

1. Work toward a comprehensive story with a beginning, middle, and end to the story, incorporating thoughts and feelings.
2. Take into the account the child's communication style and preference; this may require a social story approach (psychoeducational information about trauma; see Ch. 1 Clinical Worksheets).
3. A written trauma story may not be appropriate for a child with a communication difficulty; alternate ways in which the child may process trauma may be used. Recommendations of speech therapy, occupational therapy, or teachers can guide the design of this intervention.
4. A verbal or symbolic recounting of abusive events (expressive) can be helpful when a written narrative is not appropriate.
5. Trauma stories can be communicated through a third-person perspective (other kids' stories of their abuse) about the events and why they occurred.
6. Trauma stories can be completed in "doses," where small amounts of processing are more appropriate for individuals with greater dysregulation. This can take place over several sessions.
7. Trauma stories can also be done outside of session, in-between sessions, where narratives are continuously revised as treatment progresses. Ongoing reframing and reinterpreting of the traumatic events promotes the integration of greater aspects of the trauma that have been discovered and processed in trauma treatment.

MY TRAUMA STORY

Good work! Writing your trauma narrative is a major accomplishment! Now that you have shared your story, it can be helpful to talk with your therapist about other aspects of your trauma.

1. Discuss with your therapist your past and current relationship with the person who abused you.

2. Do you ever feel to blame for the abuse? Who is to blame for the abuse? Who is responsible for the abuse?

3. What negative feelings do you still have about the abuse? Are you or have you ever been angry at anyone for the abuse? Or for not protecting you?

4. Are there any other aspects of your trauma that you think would be important to discuss with your therapist?

SOCIAL SKILLS/HEALTHY RELATIONSHIPS WORKSHEETS

SOCIAL SKILLS/HEALTHY RELATIONSHIPS WORKSHEETS

For Clinicians: Refer to Chapter 1 as needed. Make sure to reinforce the idea that children can experience mixed feelings as well as a variety of feelings, especially related to trauma.

Remember when we learned to identify different feelings in Chapter 1? You did such a great job learning about tons of different feelings!

Remember that everyone has good and bad feelings and can have more than one feeling at once! Can you think of an example where you had more than one feeling? Draw or write your answer below:

Great job! Now, we are going to learn about how you can TALK about your feelings.

Sometimes it might be hard to let other people know how you feel, or to find the right feeling word! Especially if your feeling is VERY STRONG! It is important to help calm your feeling down so you can tell others how you feel. What are ways that you can calm your feeling and body down when your feelings get too strong?

1. ______________________________

2. ______________________________

3. ______________________________

4. ______________________________

5. ______________________________

Now that you know how to CALM your feeling down, you are ready to talk about your feeling! One way to do this is to use "I" statements. That means you start by saying "I feel __________ when__________. I need__________." This is a good way to tell someone else what you are feeling, why you are feeling that way, and what you need to feel better. LET'S PRACTICE: THINK OF SOME EXAMPLES OVER THE LAST COUPLE OF DAYS AND WRITE THEM BELOW.

I feel ______________________________

when ______________________________

I need ______________________________

I feel ______________________________

when ______________________________

I need ______________________________

I feel ______________________________

when ______________________________

I need ______________________________

It is also important to learn how to be a good friend and help others and yourself! What does being a good friend mean to you?

For Clinicians: Make sure to highlight how to show interest in others, being kind, how to borrow, being respectful, and being dependable.

Sometimes we all need help, and part of being a good friend is helping others. Can you think of an example when a friend helped you? Or when you helped a friend?

Learning a good way to ask for help is very important. The way we act and the things we say can impact other people, so learning a polite way to ask for help or respond to a friend is very important.

For Clinicians: Role-play different scenarios on appropriate ways to ask for help.

Communication Skills and Building Supportive Relationships

Clinicians: The following worksheets are designed to guide therapy discussions and teaching on topics and skills related to communication and building relationships with others. Caregivers should be included in discussions about how to support these skills outside of sessions. Please remember to modify worksheets and activities appropriately for your client.

Good communication skills is very important for any healthy relationship. The following areas are important **verbal communication skills** to have when socializing with others. Practice these in sessions with your therapist and then try using them outside of sessions. It is important to practice, practice, and practice!

1. Meeting new people and introducing yourself.
   a. Make eye contact.
   b. Smile.
   c. Say, "Hello."
   d. Say, "My name is _______________." "What is your name?"
   e. Say, "Nice to meet you."

2. Remembering names.
   a. Associating the name with an aspect of the person. For example, "Brown-haired Braden," or "Park District Paul."
   b. Rhyming names with objects you'll remember. For example, "Sarah lives near O'Hare-a,", or "Paul who plays ball."

3. Asking questions and getting to know others.
   a. Ask warm up questions first. Warm up questions are less personal questions or typical questions one might ask someone new. Examples of these questions are, "How have you been liking this weather?" or "Where did you grow up?"
   b. If warm up questions go well, then asking more personal questions and getting to know another person is a natural next step. More personal questions might be, "What do you do for fun?" or "Do you have a pet?"

4. Listening during a conversation and active listening. If you are interested in getting to know another person or making a new friend, it is important to show that you are listening to them and trying to understand them.
   a. Maintain eye contact.
   b. Repeat back some of what the person is saying to show them you are listening and to show them that you want to hear more.
   c. Take turns talking and listening.

5. Giving feedback. Sometimes when you are talking to someone, he/she may ask for your ideas. It is okay to share your ideas with them, but remember to be respectful when sharing them. If someone does not ask for your ideas about something, ask if they would like

to hear your ideas before deciding to share them. When someone has not asked for your ideas about something, it is usually not a good decision to share them.

6. Giving and accepting compliments. Compliments are usually something said to a person that makes him/her feel good. It is usually a good decision to only give compliments, or say something nice about someone, if you really mean it. This will help build a true, honest relationship with someone. If you don't have something nice to say about someone, it is usually best to not say anything to them. When someone says something nice about you, it is usually a good idea to thank them for this. If someone says something to you that makes you feel uncomfortable, then this is something you should share with someone you trust to help you talk about it.

7. Sharing and cooperating.
   a. Sharing can be difficult. Especially because it involves giving something up. Sharing can also make you feel good because you are giving your things to help others and thinking and caring about others. When others share with you, you usually feel good because someone is being nice to you or thinking about you.
   b. Cooperating means working together to complete a task. Cooperating is important because it uses more minds and can take less time to do something. It can also be fun and can help you make a new friend.

8. Following rules and making decisions.
   a. Inflexible rules. Rules are important because they tell us how to behave and be successful in social situations. Some rules are inflexible, or always have to be followed, so that people are not hurt. Other rules help people get along with each other. Inflexible rules might be no hitting others or tell the truth.
   b. Flexible rules. Some rules are flexible, or can change a little, but can change if no one is hurt. Flexible rules may include when chores need to be completed or which fun activity might be planned for the day.
   c. Making decisions. When making decisions, it is helpful to spend some time thinking about the decision being made. Sometimes listing the good reasons for you to make the decision and then listing the bad reasons for you to make the decision can help you know which decision is best for you. Some decisions may involve you losing something to gain what is best for you in the end. It is okay if you make a decision that doesn't turn out to be good for you. This bad decision will help you make a better decision the next time.

9. Accepting differences and making true friends.
   a. To get along with others, it is important to learn to accept the ways others are different from you. When we are open to others' differences, we can learn from others. One way to start this process is to be kind to others who are different and take time to get to know them. In doing this, you are accepting them and getting to know them. If you decide over time that you do not like the person or don't think they are a good friend for you, that's okay. Sometimes you need time to figure this out.

b. It is important to understand the difference between "popular" people and true friends. Some people who are considered popular may not be a true or good friend for you. When you understand what makes other people popular and you understand what a good for you is, you will be able to make a better decision about this.
c. True friends are people who like you and accept you for who you are. Think about your friends? Do they like? Do they accept you? Do you feel they look up to you?

Learning **nonverbal communication skills** is just as important as knowing communication skills in building successful relationships. Nonverbal communication skills includes not only our facial expressions, but body gestures, eye contact and even how we say what we say! Being aware of and understanding nonverbal communication skills can help your relationship with other people and can help other people better understand you! The following nonverbal behaviors can be especially helpful to know for improving your nonverbal communication skills.

For Clinicians: Work with each individual to further explain and role-play adaptive ways to utilize these nonverbal communication skills.

1. Vocal cadence, volume, and tone

2. Facial expressions and eye contact

3. Gestures

4. Personal space

5. Touch

6. Posture

7. Emotional identification and self-awareness

Being Responsible for Yourself and Others

Clinicians: The following worksheets are designed to guide therapy discussions and teaching on topics and skills related to taking responsibility for oneself and being mindful of other's feelings. Caregivers should be included in discussions about how to support these skills outside of sessions.

In this section, several areas related to being responsible for yourself and others are presented. It is important to discuss these skills with your therapist, as well as how you might see yourself doing them. How you do these skills is unique to you as an individual. People have many ways of offering help, being good to themselves, and managing stress.

When being responsible for **others**:

1. Ask for help when you need it.
2. Understand how your behavior affects others. This may require reflective listening skills that you learned in the last worksheet.
3. Try to understand others.
4. Show interest and concern for others in return.
5. Give and receive advice.
6. Be a friend.
7. Be respectful.
8. Offer help when you can.

When being responsible for **yourself**:

1. Feel good about yourself.
2. Create a positive attitude.
3. Stick up for yourself.
4. Pat yourself on the back.
5. Avoid fights.
6. Deal with teasing.

7. Identify stress.

8. Manage peer pressure.

9. Learn to say no.

10. Release anger safely.

11. Know rights and responsibilities.

12. Be assertive.

Solving Problems and Resolving Conflict

<u>Clinicians</u>: The following worksheets are designed to guide therapy discussions and teaching on topics and skills related to solving problems and resolving conflict. Caregivers should be included in discussions about how to support these skills outside of sessions.

It is important to build skills in problem-solving and conflict resolution, as these are ongoing situations you face throughout your life. Developing these skills will enhance your self-confidence and belief that you can handle things, which will increase your success as a person. Below are several skills that lead to more effective problem-solving and conflict resolution.

1. Be able to identify a problem.

2. Learn how to brainstorm solutions.

3. Learn how to decide on the best solution through identifying positive and negative outcomes.

4. Learn from mistakes.

5. Be able to think before acting.

6. Learn how to make wise choices.

7. Be able to accept consequences.

8. Learn how to apologize and resolve conflicts calmly.

9. Learn how to compromise in a way that feels right to you.

10. Learn how to negotiate.

Bullying Prevention Skills

Clinicians: The following worksheets are designed to guide therapy discussions and teaching on topics and skills related to managing bullies and bullying. Caregivers should be included in discussions about how to support these skills outside of sessions.

Bullying is a widespread epidemic across our country. You may even be or have been a target of bullying. Because of its prevalence and the potential for you to be effected by it if you haven't already been, it is important to learn more about bullying, know the signs of bullying, how to respond to bullying, and how to stop it. Below you will find information about these important topics.

1. Understand bullying. Bullies act with the intent to hurt someone, repeatedly, and chooses someone he/she perceives as vulnerable as his/her target. Bullying can be physical, verbal, relational (rumor spreading, excluding, turning people against someone), or involve the internet (cyberbullying).

2. Recognize signs of bullying. What are some of the signs of bullying experienced? Caregivers may notice that children no longer want to go to school, have damage to property, or exhibit physical ailments or symptoms. Additionally, academic performance can decrease and there may be an increase in behavioral symptoms noted (increase isolation, behaviorally acting out, etc.).

3. Learn how to respond effectively to bullying. Exhibiting self-confidence, avoiding bullying tactics, responding with assertiveness, and obtaining support from others have been found to be most effective in responding to bullying.

SEXUAL BEHAVIOR PROBLEMS WORKSHEETS

SEXUAL BEHAVIOR PROBLEMS WORKSHEETS

Many boys and girls have sexual behavior problems that they need help to stop. Sexual behavior problems might also be called sexual touching problems. Sexual behavior problems are when one person does sexual touching with another person without their permission. Sexual touching includes touching private parts. Sexual behavior problems can include more than just wrong touching. Work with your counselor to learn about different types of sexual behavior problems.

For Clinicians: Review additional behaviors such as viewing pornography, exposing oneself to others, excessive or inappropriate masturbation/self-stimulation, inappropriate sexual content during conversations, etc. Make sure to include ALL sexual behaviors identified in your client, and refer to your initial assessment/evaluation to be comprehensive. ALSO, make sure to review WHY these behaviors are inappropriate. Be sure to include caregivers in this section so that they can be informed of how to support and intervene with the client around his/her sexual behavior problems.

Many kids have lots of different feelings when they talk about sexual behaviors or sexual touching problems. Circle what feelings you are having below.

Sad

Scared

Excited

Uncomfortable

Happy

Mad

Confused

Guilty

Embarrassed

Funny

What other feelings might you have? Write or draw below:

Boys and girls, teenagers, and even adults can have sexual behavior problems. List your sexual behavior problems below (your therapist can help you with this). Then, try to think of when your sexual behavior problems started (your counselor can help you) and write this below:

Sexual behavior problems can be caused by many things such as if someone did sexual touching with you when you were younger. This can create lots of different thoughts and feelings in your body that you were too young to get. It was **NOT OKAY** if someone did sexual touching with you, just like it is **NOT OKAY** for you to do sexual touching with anyone now.

Write or draw reasons for your sexual behavior problems below (your counselor can help you):

Good job! Talking about sexual behavior problems is not an easy thing to do, but you are working really hard!

Work with your counselor now to figure out some examples of good touch and bad touch:

<u>Good touch</u>:

<u>Bad touch</u>:

What are some of the things that can happen if someone has sexual behavior problems? Or keeps doing sexual touching? What types of trouble can you get in for doing sexual behavior problems? How did you feel when you were abused? How do you think the person(s) felt that you abused? (You can use the feeling chart on the next page to help.) Write or draw your ideas below:

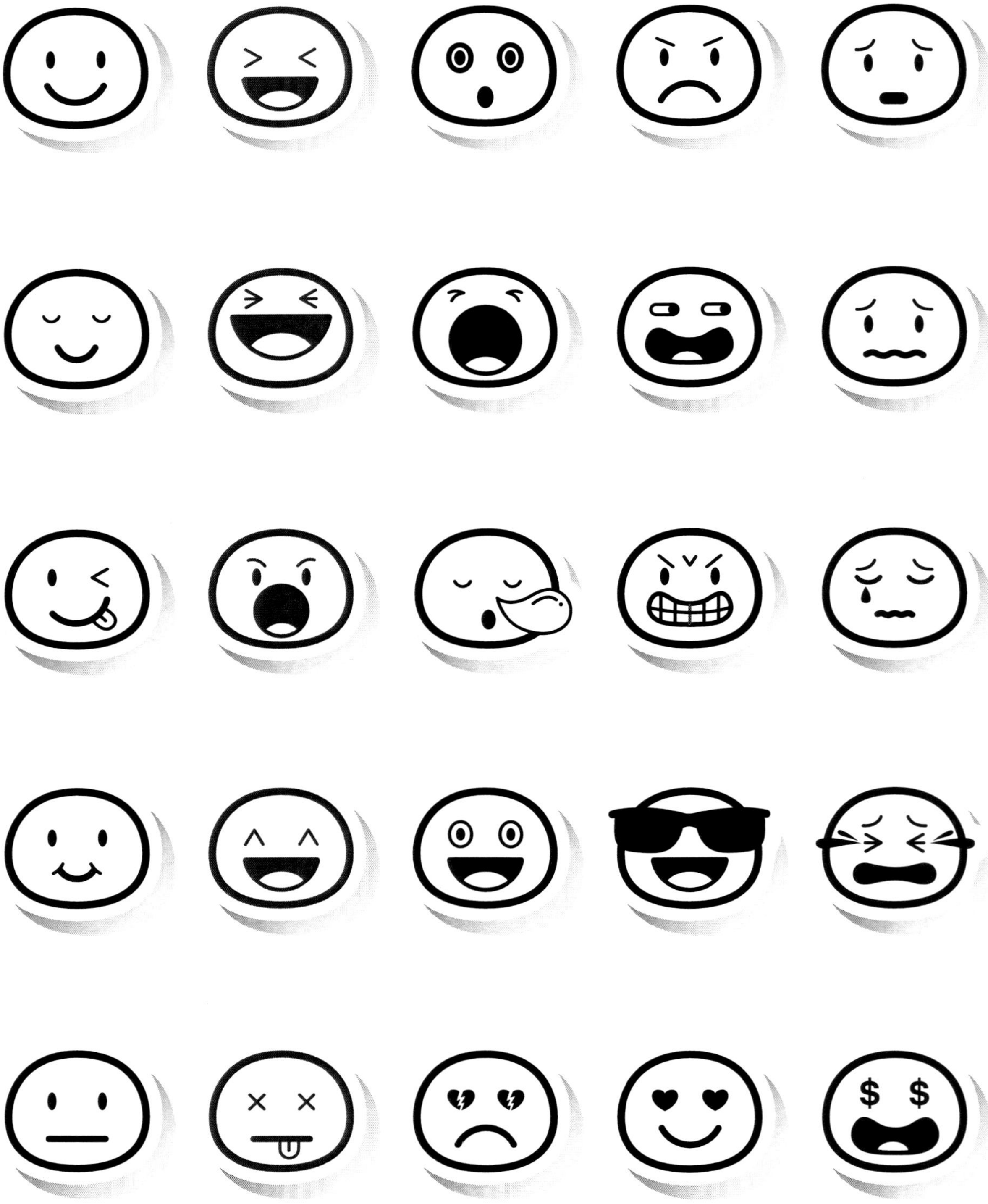

Work with your counselor to think of ways that you can stop your wrong sexual thoughts, feelings, and behaviors:

____

____

____

____

____

____

____

____

____

What is my future plan? When I start to feel_______________________ I can:

____

____

____

____

____

____

____

____

____

____

SEX EDUCATION/BODY AWARENESS WORKSHEETS

SEX EDUCATION/BODY AWARENESS WORKSHEETS

Entering Puberty

Puberty can be a stressful and confusing time, but it doesn't have to be. The following guidelines and suggested resources serve to provide some information about this important topic to help lower stress and confusion about this process.

For Clinicians: Helpful books such as resources found in the appendices, and visual aids can be helpful in facilitating this discussion. Caregivers should be given the following information. As stated previously, clinicians should modify worksheets and exercises appropriately for their client.

Guidelines for this discussion:

1. Start early in treatment with a discussion about puberty.
2. Teach specific body parts and bodily functions to avoid confusion and increase effective communication about these things later.
3. Teach specific to the individual. Teach about puberty in the way that the individual learns best. For example, some people learn better through repetition of the same information and some learn better with pictures.
4. Encourage further discussion with professionals, such as physicians, teachers, and other therapists.

Staying Active

It is important to learn how to be healthy from an early age. Some specific conditions or situations, like hormone changes with puberty or certain medications, can make it difficult to be healthy because of increased body weight that can result. A healthy diet and regular exercise can help stop weight gain and increase mood, and even how we feel about ourselves.

Things to help you stay active:

1. Schedule physical activities each day or several each week. Make a list of possible physical activities that you can look at if you need ideas. Choosing fun, active activities can help you get started more easily.

2. Discuss physical activity with your professionals. Your physician, occupational, or physical therapist may have safe, fun ideas for physical exercise. If you need accommodations, there may be resources in the community that offer adapted or supported sports activities.

3. Reward yourself for doing physical activity. Try not to reward yourself with food, which can work against the hard work you are doing. Instead, choose a reward such as, an activity you enjoy (computer game, movie, time with a friend).

Hygiene

Hygiene is important for good physical health, as well as for social wellness and personal esteem and confidence.

For Clinicians: Laminated visual aids or picture schedules can be helpful in teaching hygiene skills. Encouraging caregivers to create this with his/her child, teen, or young adult with your guidance is recommended. The number of pictures, or steps to managing hygiene, will depend on factors such as, assessing steps the child, teen, or young adult has the most difficulty and breaking down some steps with more pictures to assist him/her accordingly. Specific pictures of the shampoo bottle can be helpful for those that require more specific and detailed instruction. Creating a visual schedule with the child, teen, or young adult's input and help encourages a sense of personal responsibility and accomplishment in him/her. Organizing and labeling items needed for each hygiene task can also help the child, teen, or young adult have greater success with learning hygiene skills, while also helping them to learn to organize items for other life tasks. Make hygiene activities routine. Refer to Appendix for additional resources to guide these discussions.

Hygiene areas of focus:

1. Hair hygiene. If this is a sensitive area for you, try listening to music while you shower, use a soft sponge to wash your hair, and a cup to rinse your hair. Keeping your hair clean increases your physical health and makes you more appealing to others you come in contact with socially.

2. Body odor hygiene. As people age and reach puberty, their body changes and can cause body odor or unpleasant smells. Deodorants are used to help with this. You may need to try a couple of different deodorants until you find one you like. Scents may not appeal to you or you may be too sensitive to them. If you sweat more, you may need to have a change of clothes with you and change clothes part way through the day. It will be important to have a routine of when you do laundry to make sure you have clean clothes available. It can be helpful to mark this on a calendar. Waiting too long to do laundry can make doing laundry an overwhelming task. Depending on how often you change clothes during the week, you may need to do laundry two days a week to help manage your clothes. Keeping your body clean helps you feel good, and is more appealing to others you interact with, and enhances your social life.

3. Body hair hygiene. It is helpful for a teen or young adult to understand where body hair has developed with puberty, as well as discuss their interest in shaving his/her body hair. This is a personal choice. Consequences to different choices should be discussed with the teen or young adult so that they can make an informed decision about this. A caregiver modeling how to shave can be very helpful, and encouraging the teen or young adult to practice shaving in front of the caregiver can also be helpful. Visual aids are helpful for highlighting specific trouble areas or as reminders. Marking on a calendar when to shave (similar to a laundry schedule) and when to change razors (if applicable) can also be

helpful. Trouble areas can be using shaving cream in excess and finding a razor that works best for you, much like choosing the right deodorant.

4. Teeth hygiene. It is important to find the right toothbrush for you. You may find a soft bristle toothbrush more comfortable, or like the intensity of an electric toothbrush. It is important to know how long to spend brushing your teeth and to use a timer or small hourglass to help you with this.

5. Acne problems. Consult with your physician about over the counter products that may be beneficial, or about a stronger prescription if needed. Use caution around your eyes and mouth; a visual aid can be helpful in indicating where a product should be used. This would also apply to body acne, again consulting with you physician about body wash products for this. Feeling good about your skin can enhance self-esteem and self-confidence, and encourage greater social interaction.

Social Issues and Mood Changes

Social skills and friendships and are important to older children, teens, and young adults. Making and keeping friends, as well as feeling part of a group can be difficult and stressful. Outside appearances, such as hair, clothing, and social interests are important things to think about, as they tend to impact your social life.

Social issues to consider:

1. Extracurricular activities. Exploring groups that you think you might enjoy is a good start. This may be an organized sport, a specific club or membership to an organization, or a youth group. If you have trouble finding a group, your local advocacy group may have a list of options for you to explore or if you have an interest and the motivation, start a new group or club! When joining a team, group, or club, it is always important to share with the coach or leader any special needs you have that they should be aware of in order to best support you. If the team, group, or club is comprised of a diverse group of peers, asking about sensitivity training as part of the group activities can be helpful to enhance empathy and understanding among peers toward one another.

2. Body Odor You may need to try a couple of different deodorants until you find one you like. Scents may not appeal to you or you may be too sensitive to them. If you sweat more, you may need to have a change of clothes with you and change clothes part way through the day. It will be important to have a routine of when you do laundry to make sure you have clean clothes available. It can be helpful to mark this on a calendar. Waiting too long to do laundry can make doing laundry an overwhelming task. Depending on how often you change clothes during the week, you may need to do laundry two days a week to help manage your clothes. Keeping your body clean helps you feel good, and is more appealing to others you interact with, and enhances your social life.

3. Hair. It is helpful for a teen or young adult to understand where body hair has developed with puberty, as well as discuss their interest in shaving his/her body hair. This is a personal choice. Consequences to different choices should be discussed with the teen or young adult so that they can make an informed decision about this. A caregiver modeling how to shave can be very helpful, and encouraging the teen or young adult to practice shaving in front of the caregiver can also be helpful. Visual aids are helpful for highlighting specific trouble areas or as reminders. Marking on a calendar when to shave (similar to a laundry schedule) and when to change razors (if applicable) can also be helpful. Trouble areas can be using shaving cream in excess and finding a razor that works best for you, much like choosing the right deodorant.

4. Skin. Consult with your physician about over the counter products that may be beneficial, or about a stronger prescription if needed, if acne or skin conditions are a concern. Use caution around your eyes and mouth; a visual aid can be helpful in indicating where a product should be used. This would also apply to body acne, again consulting with

your physician about body wash products for this. Feeling good about your skin can enhance self-esteem and self-confidence, and encourage greater social interaction.

Moods and feelings can be ever changing during puberty. Learning how to express feelings is extremely important during this time. Referring to the worksheets in Chapter 1 can be helpful when identifying modulating feelings.

Warning signs of more serious mood problems.

There may be more serious mood concerns when the following are present:

Extreme or strange expression of emotions

Agitated behavior

Frequent aggression

Changes in appetite

Ongoing physical complaints

Changes in sleep

Odd thinking

Changes in energy level

Understanding Menstruation and Self-Care (for Females)

Some of the physical changes that happen to your body during puberty can be scary if they are not understood. The following information can help increase your understanding about these physical changes and help you adjust to these changes more easily.

For Clinicians: There are several suggested resources to facilitate a discussion about menstruation and other important aspects about the physical changes that accompany puberty. Taking opportunities to discuss issues related to puberty as they arise can be helpful. Using positive and encouraging statements helps communicate that you are a helpful and safe person to talk about the information. This help you become an approachable person. As mentioned in previous chapters, it is always important to give information in the best way that the receiver of information can learn it. Encouraging caregivers to include the family physician in discussions can be helpful and assist with increased comfort prior to beginning her first female exam.

1. <u>Education</u>. It is important to talk about the physical changes that will be happening to your body before they happen so that you can be best prepared. This includes learning about your menstruation cycle, including what to expect when your menstrual period comes and how to be prepared when it does.

2. <u>Practice</u>. Using sanitary napkins (pads), tampons, and wearing bras will be something very new. It can be helpful to start preparing to use these with practice to decrease any anxiety you might have, as well as help you learn how to manage these new things. It will be important to learn about how to wear and use sanitary napkins or pads and tampons, when to change them, and how to care for their disposal. If there is an appropriate female role model to demonstrate how to use these. Practicing wearing them can be helpful prior to the start of menstruation. There are varying types of pads in terms of thickness, winged, and scented or unscented. Similarly, it can be helpful to start getting used to having additional clothing or a bra under your shirt. This can be done by wearing tank tops, camisoles, or even sports bras or training bras. When you decide to start wearing bras, there are many different types, so it will be important to try on different options and find the bra that feels most comfortable to you.

3. <u>Storage</u>. It can be helpful to have a specific container to keep pads and tampons in that you carry with you, especially around the time your menstrual cycle is expected to come. It may be helpful to mark on a calendar when your menstrual period comes, so that you can plan for the next one.

4. <u>The female or gynecological exam</u>. In preparing for the female exam, visiting the doctor's office you will be going to can help. Getting a tour of the office and exam rooms, and learning about what will happen during the exam will help you know what to expect. Bringing something relaxing with you on the day of your exam may be comforting to you. Be sure to plan something enjoyable after your exam. Finally, it is important for you to find a doctor who you feel comfortable sharing personal information with and who is willing to hear you and answer your questions, as well as address your concerns.

5. Menstrual issues or concerns. Some women experience extremely painful menstrual cycles. Be sure to consult with you doctor about this, as there may be medications that you can take to relieve the pain or regulate your menstrual cycle in a way that results in less pain. If your doctor does prescribe medication for you, it is always important to follow the instructions for how to take the medication to get the best results.

Understanding Your Private Parts (for Males)

During puberty, there are some natural processes that involve your private parts, specifically your penis, which you should know about so that you understand what is happening to you.

Underwear Choices

There are different types of underwear from which to choose. There are tighter fitting briefs and looser fitting boxers. Boxers are more like shorts and can be easier to dress, whereas briefs are tighter fitting and provide more support to your private parts. Because these choices are so different, it may be helpful to try each on, and you may even find an underwear choice in-between these that you like better. Underwear is a personal choice and it is important that you find the right match for you so that you feel comfortable throughout the day.

Nocturnal Emissions

It is common for the penis to release semen, which is a liquid that contains sperm, while you are sleeping. Sometimes you may wake up wet or notice wet areas on your bed or underwear and pajamas. It is important to understand the difference between wetting or peeing in your bed and having nocturnal emissions while sleeping. When you are aware of this, you may feel less embarrassed or shameful about it and may be more willing to discuss this with an adult you trust.

It is helpful to learn what you can do after a nocturnal emission has happened, such as how to clean your sheets, your clothing, and yourself. If you the need the help of your caregiver, it will be important to find a way to communicate with them about what happened, or to have a special way to refer to needing help with a nocturnal emission. Just like your private parts are a private matter, so are the things your private parts do. Talking to adults who you have identified as helpers about your concerns is best. If one of your helpers has a negative reaction to you, talk to another helper until you feel you have gotten your concerns addressed. Remember, you can always ask your doctor about your body and your body's processes.

Erections

It is also common for the penis to have many erections throughout the day. Many times, this happens without your control. Because you can't avoid them, they may happen during a time you may feel embarrassed by it. There are some things you can do when you have an erection at an uncomfortable time. If you are carrying something, you can move it in front of your pants to cover your private part area until it goes away. If you aren't carrying something, but have an additional piece of clothing around you, you can tie it around your waist or hold it in front of your private part area. If you are already sitting, you can stay seated until it passes. Finally, your choice of underwear can help hide erections. Close-fitting brief underwear may hold your penis closer to your body and make the erection less noticeable. If briefs are not comfortable to you, this may not be an option for you.

SAFETY SKILLS TRAINING WORKSHEETS

SAFETY SKILLS TRAINING WORKSHEETS

Many kids, teenagers, and adults who experience sexual abuse may feel unsafe or worried about their safety, even after the abuse has stopped. It is very normal to feel this way.

In what ways do you feel unsafe?

In what ways do you feel safe?

There are important tools to learn to help keep you and your body safe. What can you do if you start to feel unsafe? (You can ask your counselor for help.)

Safe helpers are adults or other people in your life you can go to if you need help or you feel unsafe. Examples might be your mom, teacher, or counselor. Who are your safe helpers?

What can you do if someone tries to abuse you again, or tries to trick you into doing something that you do not want to do?

For Clinicians: Include caregivers in ways they can help keep their child safe. Review and repeat the information in these worksheets with the client throughout treatment.

For Caregivers:

Ways to keep your child safe:

1. *Talk to your child early.* Help your child learn the difference between public and private behaviors and make appropriate rules in your home. Examples may include taking a bath or shower alone. Visual reminders can be helpful for some children.
2. *Use Examples.* Children love stories! There are many wonderful, age-appropriate stories, books, and resources available that discuss ways to stay safe. A caregiver or clinician can create an individualized story for your child regarding a specific behavior or setting.
3. *Redirect and reframe.* If your child engages in any inappropriate behaviors or behaviors in an inappropriate context (such as touching oneself in public) then make sure to redirect them to a more appropriate behavior or setting.
4. *Plan ahead.* If your child requires help with toileting, dressing, etc. make sure to discuss what is appropriate and not appropriate (such as who can help them) and how they can ask for help from approved caregivers or adults.
5. (Please include anything additional that is unique to your child.): ____________________

____

Appendix

ADDITIONAL RESOURCES

I. Resources to Guide Trauma Treatment Sessions

A. For Children

1. *Red flag/green flag people: ABC's of personal safety for preschool aged children* (ages 3-5) by Red Flag Green Flag Resources. (http://www.redflag-greenflag.com/index.html)
2. *Red flag/green flag people: A personal safety program for early elementary aged children* (ages 5-8) by Red Flag Green Flag Resources. (http://www.redflaggreenflag.com/index.html)
3. *Red flag/green flag people II: A sexual abuse prevention program for older elementary aged children* (ages 8-11) by Red Flag Green Flag Resources. (http://www.redflaggreenflag.com/index.html)
4. S*teps to healthy touching: Activities to help kids understand and control their problems with touching.* (Macfarlane & Cunningham)
5. *Treatment Exercises for child abuse victims and children with sexual behavior problems.* (Cavanagh-Johnson)
6. *Paper dolls and paper airplanes: Therapeutic exercises for sexually traumatized children.* (Crisci, Lay, & Lowenstein)
7. *Annie and Andy Storybooks for children who have been sexually abused.* (ages 4-8) by Red Flag Green Flag Resources. (http://www.redflaggreenflag.com/index .html)
8. *Flip Flops: A workbook for children who have been sexually abused.* (ages 7-9) (Spinal-Robinson & Baldwin)
9. *Cartwheels: A workbook for children who have been sexually abused.* (ages 10-13) (Spinal-Robinson & Baldwin)
10. *Feeling good again: A workbook for children who have been sexually abused.* (ages 6 and up) (Wasserman & Bear)
11. *I wish the hitting would stop: A workbook for children living in violent homes.* (ages 6-14) by Red Flag Green Flag Resources. (http://www.redflag-greenflag.com/index.html)
12. *I wish the hitting would stop: A domestic violence education program for 4th and 5th graders* (approx. ages 8-11) by Red Flag Green Flag Resources. (http://www .redflaggreenflag.com/index.html)

B. For Adolescents:

1. *Treatment Exercises for child abuse victims and children with sexual behavior problems.* (Cavanagh-Johnson)
2. *Paper dolls and paper airplanes: Therapeutic exercises for sexually traumatized children.* (Crisci, Lay, & Lowenstein)
3. *High Tops: A workbook for teenagers who have been sexually abused* (ages 14-17, for age 13, see Cartwheels workbook). (Spinal-Robinson & Baldwin)
4. *Feeling good again: A workbook for children who have been sexually abused* (ages 6 and up). (Wasserman & Bear)
5. *The PTSD Workbook: Simple, effective techniques for overcoming traumatic stress symptoms* (good for older adolescents). (Williams & Poijula)
6. *I wish the hitting would stop: A workbook for children living in violent homes* (ages 6-14) by Red Flag Green Flag Resources. (http://www.redflag-greenflag .com/index.html)
7. *Asking about sex and growing up: A question-and-answer book for boys and girls* (puberty). (Cole)

II. Resources Specific for DD Populations

A. *Early Communication Skills for Children with Down Syndrome* by Kumin.
B. *Essentials of Autism Spectrum Disorders Evaluation and Assessment* by Saulnier and Ventola.
C. *Essentials of Specific Learning Disability Identification* by Flanagan and Alfonso.
D. *Helping a Child with Nonverbal Learning Disorder or Asperger's Syndrome* by Stewart.
E. *Learning Disabilities* by McBee Knox.
F. *Understanding Cerebral Palsy: A Guide for Parents and Professionals* by Stanton.
G. *A Picture's Worth: Pecs and Other Visual Communication Strategies in Autism* by Bondy and Frost.
H. *Autism-Asperger's & Sexuality: Puberty and Beyond* by Newport.
I. *Social Skills Training* by Baker.
J. *The New Social Story Book* by Gray.

III. General Resources

1. *Ready...set...R.E.L.A.X.: A research-based program of relaxation, learning, and self-esteem for children* by Jeff Allen, MA, and Roger Klein, PsyD.
2. *Another chance to get it right* by Andrew Vachss.
3. *The Berenstain bears and the trouble with friends* by Stan Berenstain and Jan Berenstain.
4. *The Berenstain bears get in a fight* by Stan Berenstain and Jan Berenstain.
5. *The Berenstain bears learn about strangers* by Stan Berenstain and Jan Berenstain.

6. *Skills training for children with behavior problems, revised edition: A parent and practitioner guidebook* by Michael Bloomquist, PhD.
7. *It's MY body: A book to teach young children how to resist uncomfortable touch* by Lory Britain, PhD.
8. *The sexual abuse victim and sexual offender treatment planner* by Arthur Jonhsma, Jr., PhD and Rita Budrionis, PsyD.
9. *The way I feel* by Janan Cain.
10. *Paper dolls and paper airplanes: Therapeutic exercises for sexually traumatized children* by Geraldine Crisci, MSW, Marilynn Lay, MSW, and Liana Lowenstein, MSW, RSW, CPT-S.
11. *Red flag green flag people: A personal safety program for children and coloring book* by Kecia Softing Freed.
12. *Healthy bodies: A parent's guide on puberty for boys with disabilities* by Vanderbilt Kennedy Center.
13. *Healthy bodies: A parent's guide on puberty for girls with disabilities* by Vanderbilt Kennedy Center.
14. *For kids only: A guide to safety and sexual abuse prevention* by Catalina Herrerias, Ph.D, MSW.
15. *A terrible thing happened* by Margaret Holmes, Sasha Mudlaff, and Cary Pillo
16. *Please tell: A child's story about sexual abuse* by Jessie. Published by Hazelden. July 1, 1991.
17. *104 activities that build: Self-esteem, teamwork, communication, anger management, self-discovery, coping skills* by Alanna Jones
18. *Pathways: A guided workbook for youth beginning treatment* by Timothy Kahn.
19. *Bridging worlds: Understanding and facilitating adolescent recovery from the trauma of abuse* by Joycee Kennedy and Carol McCarthy.
20. *Answers to questions teachers ask about sensory integration: Forms, checklists, and practical tools for teachers and parents* by Carol Kranowitz, MA, Jane Koomar, PhD, OTR/L, FAOTA, Stacey Szklut, MS, OTR/L, Lynn Balzer-Martin, PhD, OTR, Elizabeth Haber, MS, OTR/L, and Deanna Iris Sava, MS, OTR/L.
21. *How to be a friend: A guide to making friends and keeping them (Dino Life Guides for Families)* by Laurie Krasny Brown and Marc Brown.
22. *Don't pop your cork on Mondays! The children's anti-stress book.* by Adolph Moser, Ed.D., and Dav Pilkey.
23. *A leader's guide to we can get along: A child's book of choices* by Lauren Murphy Payne, MSW, and Claudia Rohling, MSW.
24. *Amazing you!: Getting smart about your private parts* by Gail Saltz, M.D., and Lynne Avril Cravath.
25. *The care and keeping of friends (American Girl Library)* by Sally Seamans and Nadine Bernard Westcott.
26. *101 ways to teach children social skills: A ready-to-use reproducible activity book.* U.S.A: Retrieved from http://www.socialskillscentral.com/free/101 _Ways_Teach_Children_Social_Skills.pdf
27. *The very angry day that Amy didn't have* by Lawrence E. Shapiro, Ph.D., and Charles Brenna.

28. *Brave Bart: A story for traumatized and grieving children* by Caroline H. Sheppard, ACSW.
29. *The saddest time* by Norma Simon and Jacqueline Rogers.
30. *Eyes on bullying...what can you do?: A toolkit to prevent bullying in children's lives.* Retrieved from http://melissainstitute.org/documents/Slaby-Prevention _toolkit.pdf
31. Van Bourgondien, M.E., Reichle, N.C., & Palmer, A. (1997). Sexual behavior in adults with autism. *Journal of Autism and Developmental Disorders, 27*(2), 113-125.
32. *Ready-to-Use social skills lessons & activities for grades 4-6* by The Society for Prevention of Violence with The Center for Applied Research in Education (Edited by Ruth Weltmann Begun).
33. *YogaKids: Educating the whole child through yoga* by Marsha Wenig, CYT, and Susan Andrews (photographer).
34. *What you need to know about dating violence: A teen's handbook* (Liz Caliborne Women's Work. (2000) Retrieved from http://www.loveisrespect.org/resources/teen_handbook.pdf
35. *Yikes! A smart girl's guide to surviving tricky, sticky, icky situations* by American Girl Editorial Staff, Bonnie Timmons, and Nancy Holyoke.

REFERENCES

101 ways to teach children social skills: A ready-to-use reproducible activity book. U.S.A: Retrieved from http://www.socialskillscentral.com/free/101_Ways_Teach_Children_Social_Skills.pdf

American Psychiatric Association. (2000). *Diagnostic and statistical manual of mental disorders: DSM-IV-TR.* Washington, DC: American Psychiatric Association.

American Psychiatric Association. (2013). *Diagnostic and statistical manual of mental disorders* (5th ed.). Washington, DC: American Psychiatric Association.

Briere, J. & Lanktree, C. (2012). *Treating complex trauma in adolescents and young sdults.* United States of America. Thousand Oaks; CA: Sage Publications.

Cohen, J., Mannarino, A., & Deblinger, E. (2006). *Treating trauma and traumatic grief in children and adolescents.* New York; NY: The Guildford Press.

Eckenrode, J., Laird, M., & Doris, J. (1993). School performance and disciplinary problems among abused and neglected children. *Developmental Psychology, 29,* 53-62. doi: 10.1037/0012-1649.29.1.53

Feiring, C., Simon, V., & Cleland, C. (2009). Childhood sexual abuse, stigmatization, internalizing symptoms, and the development of sexual difficulties and dating aggression. *Journal of Consulting and Clinical Psychology, 77*(1), 127-137. doi:10.1037/a0013475

Gobin, R., & Freyd, J. (2009). Betrayal and revictimization: Preliminary findings. *Psychological Trauma: Theory, Research, Practice, and Policy, 1*(3), 242-257. doi:10.1037/a0017469

Haugaard, J. (2000). The challenge of defining child sexual abuse. *American Psychologist, 55*(9), 1036-1039. doi:10.1037/0003-066X.55.9.1036

Hund, A., & Espelage, D. (2005). Childhood sexual abuse, disordered eating, alexithymia, and general distress: A mediation model. *Journal of Counseling Psychology, 52*(4), 559-573. doi:10.1037/0022-0167.52.4.559

Jacobi, C., Hayward, C., de Zwaan, M., Kraemer, H., & Agras, W. (2004). Coming to terms with risk factors for eating disorders: Application of risk terminology and suggestions for a general taxonomy. *Psychological Bulletin, 130*(1), 19-65. doi:10.1037/0033-2909.130.1.19

Kallstrom-Fuqua, A., Weston, R., & Marshall, L. (2004). Childhood and adolescent sexual abuseof community women: Mediated effects on psychological distress and social relationships. *Journal of Consulting Psychology, 72,* 980-992. doi: 10.1037/0022-006x.72.6.980

Kaplow, J., & Widom, C. (2007). Age of onset of child maltreatment predicts long-term mental health outcomes. *Journal of Abnormal Psychology, 116*(1), 176-187. doi:10.1037/0021-843X.116.1.176

Lanktree, C., & Briere, J. (2008). *Integrative treatment of complex trauma for children (ITCT-C): A guide for treatment of multiply-traumatized children aged eight to twelve years.* Long Beach, CA: Presented by MCAVIC-USC on 10/22-23, 2008 by National Child Traumatic Stress Network (NCTSN). Learning Community Meeting.

McCarthy, J. (2001). Post-traumatic stress disorder in people with learning disability. Advances in Psychiatric Treatment, 7, 163-169.

National Child Traumatic Stress Network. (2004). *Facts on traumatic stress and children with developmental disabilities.* Retrieved from http:www.nctsn.org

Read, J., Agar, K., Barker-Collo, S., Davies, E., & Moskowitz, A. (2001). Assessing suicidality in adults: Integrating childhood trauma as a major risk factor. *Professional Psychology: Research and Practice, 32*(4), 367-372. doi:10.1037/0735-7028.32.4.367

Rodriguez, N., Ryan, S., Vande Kemp, H., & Foy, D. (1997). Posttraumatic stress disorder in adult female survivors of child sexual abuse: A comparison study. *Journal of Consulting and Clinical Psychology, 65*(1), 53-59. doi: 10.1037/0022-006X.65.1.53

Russell, A., Shah, B. (2003). Posttraumatic stress disorder and abuse. *Developmental Disabilities Digest, 30*(2) 1-8.

Ryan, R. (1994). Posttraumatic stress disorder in persons with developmental disabilities. *Community Mental Health Journal, 30*(1), 45-54.

Sachs-Ericsson, N., Blazer, D., Plant, E., & Arnow, B. (2005). Childhood sexual and physical abuse and the 1-year prevalence of medical problems in the national comorbidity survey. *Health Psychology, 24*(1), 32-40. doi:10.1037/0278-6133.24.1.32

Sobsey, D., (1996). *Relative victimization risk rates: People with intellectual disabilities.* Unpublished manuscript.

Sobsey, D. & Doe, T. (1991). Patterns of sexual abuse and assault. *Sexuality and Disability, 9*(3), 243-259.

Spatz Widam, C., Marmorstein, N., & Raskin White, H. (2006). Childhood victimization and illicit drug use in middle adulthood. *Psychology of Addictive Behaviors, 20*(4), 394-403. doi:10.1037/0893-164X.20.4.394

Storey, K., Slaby, R., Adler, M., Minotti, J., & Katz, R. (2013) *Eyes on bullying...what can you do?: A toolkit to prevent bullying in children's lives.* Newton, MA: Educational Development Center. Retrieved from http://melissainstitute.org/documents/Slaby _Prevention_toolkit.pdf

Sullivan, P., & Knutson, J., (1998). The association between child maltreatment and disabilities in a hospital-based epidemiologic study. *Child Abuse and Neglect, 22*(4), 271-288.

Testa, M., Hoffman, J., & Livingston, J. (2010). Alcohol and sexual risk behaviors as mediators of the sexual victimization–revictimization relationship. *Journal of Consulting and Clinical Psychology, 78*(2), 249-259. doi:10.1037/a0018914

Testa, M., VanZile-Tamsen, C., & Livingston, J. (2005). Childhood sexual abuse, relationship satisfaction, and sexual risk taking in a community sample of women. *Journal of Consulting and Clinical Psychology, 73*(6), 1116-1124. doi:10.1037/0022-006X.73.6.1116

TF-CBT online training module. Retrieved from http://tfcbt.musc.edu/

Townsend, C., & Rheingold, A.A., (2013). *Estimating a child sexual abuse prevalence rate for practitioners: A review of child sexual abuse prevalence studies.* Charleston, S.C., Darkness to Light. Retrieved from www.D2L.org.

Van Bourgondien, M.E., Reichle, N.C., & Palmer, A. (1997). Sexual behavior in adults with autism. *Journal of Autism and Developmental Disorders, 27*(2), 113-125.

Weierich, M., & Nock, M. (2008). Posttraumatic stress symptoms mediate the relation between childhood sexual abuse and nonsuicidal self-injury. *Journal of Consulting and Clinical Psychology, 76*(1), 39-44. doi: 10.1037/0022-006X.76.1.39

Weitlauf, A., White, S., Yancy, O., Harland, E., Van Tran, C., et al. (2013). *Healthy bodies: A parent's guide on puberty for boys with disabilities.* by Vanderbilt Leadership Education in Neurodevelopment Disabilities, Kennedy Center. Retrieved from http://kc.vanderbilt.edu/healthybodies/

Weitlauf, A., White, S., Yancy, O., Harland, E., Van Tran, C., et al. (2013). *Healthy bodies: A parent's guide on puberty for girls with disabilities.* by Vanderbilt Leadership Education in Neurodevelopment Disabilities, Kennedy Center. Retrieved from http://kc.vanderbilt.edu/healthybodies/

Westat Inc. (1993). *A report on the maltreatment of children with disabilities.* Washington, D.C.: U.S. Department of Health and Human Services.

Wilgosh, L. (1993). Sexual abuse of children with disabilities: Intervention and treatment issues for parents. *Developmental Disabilities Bulletin, 21*(2). Retrieved 10/26/2005 from http://www.ualberta.ca/~jpdasddc/bulletin/articles/wilgosh1993.html.

World Health Organization. (2002). *Chapter 6: Sexual violence.* Geneva, Retrieved from www.who.org

Wyatt, G., & Newcomb, M. (1990). Internal and external mediators of women's sexual abuse in childhood. *Journal of Consulting and Clinical Psychology, 58*(6), 758-767. doi:10.1037/0022-006X.58.6.758

INDEX

A

Academic and vocational problems, 12
Accepting Your Feelings Worksheet, 77
Active Tools to Calm Down Worksheet, 78
ADHD, 17, 20
Adjunct treatments and services, 43–47. *See also* Trauma treatment with children, adolescents, and young adults with DD (TT-CAYDD)
Advocacy, 41
Affect regulation, 32, 36
Affect Regulation Worksheets, 71–79
Age, 9, 12–13, 28
Alexthymia, 11
Animal-assisted therapy, 46
Anxiety, 10, 17, 37–38, 113. *See also* Posttraumatic stress disorder (PTSD)
Appendix, 163–166
Assessment and treatment guidelines, 19–26
Attention Deficit/Hyperactivity Disorder (ADHD), 17, 20
Autism Spectrum Disorder, 17

B

Behavioral difficulties
  as ADHD component, 17
  age at time of abuse and, 9
  exacerbation of, 21
  externalized, 5
  resulting from being bullied, 133
  at school, 12–13
  sexual behavior problems, 35–36
  Sexual Behavior Problems Worksheets, 135–143
Behavioral signs of stress, 76
Best practices, 23, 27
Bibliotherapy, 33
Body awareness, 36–37, 75–76, 96–97, 107–108. *See also* Hygiene; Sex education
Body Awareness Worksheets, 145–155
Borderline intellectual functioning (BIF), 15
Breathing tools, 78, 109
Bullying Prevention Skills Worksheet, 133

C

Calming tools, 78
Caregiver involvement in therapy. *See also* Family system
  for hygiene skills, 149
  information about puberty, 147
  safety training for, 161
  sexual behavior intervention, 137
  supporting outside of session skill development, 126, 130, 133
  trauma story role, 113
Caregivers, 39–42, 44, 49
Child abuse reporting, 19
Cognitive assessment, 15, 21–22. *See also* Psychological testing
Cognitive components of TT-CAYDD, 32–33
Cognitive Worksheets, 81–98
Collaboration. See Multidisciplinary approach
Communication disorders, 6, 17. *See also* Speech therapy
Communication Skills and Building Supportive Relationships Worksheets, 126–129
Complex trauma, 28, 37, 113
Conflict resolution, 132
Control issues, 11
Coping skills, 33–34, 78
Coping Skills Worksheets, 99–103

D

Dating aggression, 14
Depression, 9
Developmental disabilities (DD), vii–viii, 6–7, 15–18, 20
Developmental issues in treatment, 26
Diagnostic and Statistical Manual DSM-IV-TR and DSM 5 (APA), 17, 21
Disordered eating, 11. *See also* Nutrition concerns
Distraction, 88–89

Domestic violence, 14

E

Eating disorders, 11
Emotional numbness, 10–11
Encopresis, 8
Enuresis, 8
Erections, 155
Evaluation and testing, 19–20, 23, 43
Exercise, 148
Exposure techniques, 113
Extracurricular activities, 151

F

Family support, 41–42
Family system, 20, 24, 44. *See also* Caregiver involvement in therapy
Feelings. *See also* Mood changes and social issues
  accepting, 77
  alexthymia, 11
  worksheets for identifying, 73–74, 90, 92, 123–124, 137–138, 141–142
Fetal alcohol effects/syndrome, 17–18
Forensics, 19
Friendship, 125–129

G

Group therapy, 42–44
Guided imagery, 78
Guilt, 12

H

Healthy habits, 148
Human Immunodeficiency Virus (HIV), 8
Hygiene, 149–154. *See also* Body awareness

I

Identifying feelings. *See under* Feelings
Individualized Education Plans (IEP), 40–41
Integrative Treatment of Complex Trauma (ITCT), 28
Internalized issues, 5. *See also* specific issues i.e., guilt
Interviewing survivors, 22
Intimate relationships, 13–14

J

Journaling, 103

M

Mandated reporting, 19
Massage, 46–47
Medical problems related to sexual abuse, 5, 8
Medical services, 45–46
Medication, 44
Menstruation and self-care, 153–154. *See also* Puberty
Mindfulness, 34, 78
Mindfulness Worksheets, 108–110
Mood changes and social issues, 151–152. *See also* Feelings
Multidisciplinary approach, 18, 20–21, 24–25, 113
Muscle relaxation, 78

N

National Child Traumatic Stress Network, 6–7
Nocturnal emissions, 155
Nonsuicidal self-injury (NSSI), 10–11
Nonverbal communication skills, 129
Nutrition concerns, 46, 148. *See also* Disordered eating

O

Occupational therapy, 44–45

P

Physical abuse, 8, 10
Physical therapy, 44–45
Posttraumatic Stress Disorder (PTSD), 10–11, 13–14. *See also* Anxiety
Practice, 27–28
Pregnancy, 7–8
Preventing sexual abuse, 48–49
Problem-Solving and Resolving Conflict Worksheet, 132
Problems-to-Component Grid (PCG) for ITCT, 28
Protective factors, 14
Psychiatric services and level of care (LOC), 44
Psychoeducation
  modules, vii
  in prevention programs, 48–49
  in trauma treatment, 24, 27–29
  in TT-CAYDD, 31–32, 36
Psychoeducation Worksheets, 57–70
Psychological distress, 9, 11
Psychological testing, 19–20, 23, 43. *See also*

Cognitive assessment
Psychosocial stressors, 21
Puberty, 147, 153–156. *See also* Menstruation and self-care

R

Relaxation tools, 78
Release of information, 22, 41, 44, 46
Responsibility, 130–131
Revictimization, 10, 13

S

Safety skills training, 23, 24, 32, 37, 49
Safety Skills Training Worksheets, 157–162
School counselors, 45
School services, 20, 25, 40–41
Self-awareness and mindfulness, 34
Self-Awareness and Mindfulness Worksheets, 105–110
Self-blame, 12, 14. *See also* Stigmatization
Self-care for caregivers, 39–40
Sensory stimuli, 25, 29
Sex education, 36–37, 75–76, 153–155. *See also* Body awareness
Sex Education Worksheets, 145–155
Sexual abuse (SA) and trauma, 5–14
  academic and vocational problems, 12, 17
  anxiety and posttraumatic stress disorder (PTSD), 10–11, 13–14, 17
  behavioral difficulties resulting from, 5, 9, 12–13
  defining sexual abuse, 5–6
  depression and suicidality, 9, 14
  disordered eating, 11
  effects of, 5–14
  guilt and shame, 6, 9, 12
  intimate relationships effects, 13–14
  nonsuicidal self-injury (NSSI), 10–11
  pregnancy, STIs, and general medical concerns, 7–8
  prevalence of, 6–7
  protective factors, 14
  psychological distress, 9, 11
  revictimization, 10, 13
  risk factors, 6–7, 10
  substance abuse, 10, 13
Sexual Abuse (SA) and Trauma Worksheet, 67
Sexual Behavior Problems Worksheets, 135–143
Sexuality and sexual behavior problems, 35–36, 48
Sexually transmitted infections (STIs), 8
Shame, 6, 9, 12
Sleep, 8, 44
Social issues and mood changes, 151–152
Social skills/healthy relationships, 34–35
Social Skills/Healthy Relationships Worksheets, 121–133
Social skills treatment, 25
Social stories, 33, 113
Social workers, 45
Speech therapy, 45. *See also* Communication disorders
Stigmatization, 13–14. *See also* Self-blame
Strengths-based assessment, 20
Stress, 76
Substance abuse, 10, 13
Suicidality, 9

T

Trauma-Focused Cognitive-Behavioral Treatment (TF-CBT), 27–28
Trauma-informed assessment, 19–23
Trauma-informed treatment, 23–26
Trauma story, 37–38
Trauma Story Worksheets, 111–120
Trauma treatment models, 27–28
Trauma treatment preparation, 29–30
Trauma treatment with children, adolescents, and young adults with DD (TT-CAYDD), 31–38. *See also* Adjunct treatments and services
  affect regulation in, 32, 36
  cognitive components of, 32–33
  coping skills, 33–34, 36
  overview of, 31
  psychoeducation in, 31–32, 36
  safety skill training, 37
  sex education/body awareness, 36–37
  sexuality and sexual behavior problems, 35–36
  social skills/healthy relationship development, 34–35
  trauma story, 37–38

V

Visualization, 78
Vocational problems, 12

W

Worksheets, actvities and interventions for TT-CAYDD
  Affect Regulation, 71–79
  Cognitive Worksheets, 81–98
  Coping Skills, 99–103
  introduction to, 53

Psychoeducation Worksheets, 57–70
Safety Skills Training Worksheets, 157–162
Self-Awareness and Mindfulness Worksheets, 105–110
Sex Education/Body Awareness Worksheets, 145–155
Sexual Behavior Problems Worksheets, 135–143
Social Skills/Healthy Relationships Worksheets, 121–133
Trauma Story Worksheets, 111–120
World Health Organization, 6

Y

Yoga, 46–47